# The Future of Israel

by
John MacArthur, Jr.

MOODY PRESS
CHICAGO

©1991 by
The Moody Bible Institute
of Chicago

All Scripture quotations, unless noted otherwise, are from the *New Scofield
Reference Bible*, King James Version. Copyright © 1967 by Oxford Universi-
ty Press, Inc. Reprinted by permission.

ISBN: 0-8024-5329-5

1 2 3 4 5 Printing/LC/Year 95 94 93 92 91

*Printed in the United States of America*

# Contents

These Bible studies are taken from messages delivered by Pastor-Teacher John MacArthur, Jr., at Grace Community Church in Sun Valley, California. The recorded messages themselves may be purchased as a series or individually. Please request the current price list by writing to:

"GRACE TO YOU"
P.O. Box 4000
Panorama City, CA 91412

Or call the following toll-free number:
1-800-55-GRACE

# 1
## Israel's Future—Part 1

### Outline

Introduction
A. The Amazing Prophecy
B. Its Historical Setting
C. The Concern of Daniel

Lesson
I. The Prayer Preceding the Revelation (v. 20)
   A. Daniel's Commitment to Prayer
   B. Daniel's Method of Prayer
     1. It was in response to God's Word
     2. It was according to God's will
     3. It was fervent
     4. It included self-denial
     5. It focused on others
     6. It included corporate confession of sin
     7. It presupposed dependence on God
     8. It glorified God
II. The Messenger of the Revelation (vv. 21-23)
   A. Who He Was
   B. The Message He Brought
   C. The Time He Came
   D. The Love He Expressed
III. The Content of the Revelation (vv. 24-27)
   A. God's Purpose in History (v. 24)
     1. Stated in a negative sense

    *a*)  "To finish the transgression"
    *b*)  "To make an end of sins"
    *c*)  "To make reconciliation for iniquity"
  2. Stated in a positive sense
    *a*)  "To bring in everlasting righteousness"
    *b*)  "To seal up the vision and prophecy"
    *c*)  "To anoint the Most Holy"

Conclusion

## Introduction

A. The Amazing Prophecy

Some scholars consider Daniel 9:20-27 the single greatest defense of the divine inspiration of the Bible, for it precisely states when the Messiah would come to earth. Sir Isaac Newton, who wrote a discourse on the topic, said we could stake the truth of Christianity on that prophecy alone, made five centuries before Christ.

The prophet Daniel stated, "While I was speaking, and praying, and confessing my sin and the sin of my people, Israel . . . the [angel] Gabriel . . . said, O Daniel, . . . Seventy weeks are determined upon thy people and upon thy holy city, to finish the transgression, and to make an end of sins, and to make reconciliation for iniquity, and to bring in everlasting righteousness, and to seal up the vision and prophecy, and to anoint the most Holy. Know, therefore, and understand, that from the going forth of the commandment to restore and to build Jerusalem unto the Messiah, the Prince, shall be seven weeks, and threescore and two weeks; the street shall be built again, and the wall, even in troublous times. And after threescore and two weeks shall Messiah be cut off, but not for himself; and the people of the prince that shall come shall destroy the city and the sanctuary, and the end of it shall be with a flood, and unto the end of the war desolations are determined. And he shall confirm the covenant with many for one week; and in the midst of the week he shall cause the

8

sacrifice and the oblation to cease, and for the over-spreading of abominations he shall make it desolate, even until the consummation, and that determined shall be poured upon the desolate."

B. Its Historical Setting

After the reign of Solomon the kingdom of Israel was divided into two parts: the northern kingdom of Israel and the southern kingdom of Judah. In approximately 722 B.C. the Assyrians took away most of the inhabitants of the northern kingdom. They were dispersed in the Assyrian Empire, and few returned.

The inhabitants of the southern kingdom of Judah were later taken captive by the Babylonians—the first of four great Gentile world empires: Babylon, Medo-Persia, Greece, and Rome (cf. Dan. 7:1-8). That captivity began about 605 B.C. when King Nebuchadnezzar started what became a series of three significant deportations from Judah. In the first deportation Nebuchadnezzer carried away the young men from among the nobles and princes of Judah. Among them were four young men named Daniel, Mishael, Hananiah, and Azariah. The Babylonians renamed them Belteshazzar, Shadrach, Meshach, and Abednego (Dan. 1:6-7). Although a captive, Daniel remained fully committed to the God of Israel. As a result of his commitment and the quality of his character, he eventually became the prime minister of Babylon.

At the time the prophecy recorded in Daniel 9 was given, the Babylonian Empire had fallen to the Medo-Persian Empire. A king named Cyrus (also titled Darius) was in power. Although the Jewish exiles were now the captives of the Medo-Persians, Daniel retained his position as prime minister because of his integrity. Some scholars believe Daniel received his revelation in the year 537 B.C., which was just about seventy years after Daniel had been taken captive.

## C. The Concern of Daniel

That seventy-year mark was important to Daniel: "I . . . understood by books the number of the years, concerning which the word of the Lord came to Jeremiah, the prophet, that he would accomplish seventy years in the desolations of Jerusalem" (Dan. 9:2). Jeremiah prophesied that the people from Judah would be in captivity for seventy years (Jer. 25:11; 29:10). Daniel knew that if the seventy-year period began with the first deportation, it was nearly over (though he didn't know if the seventy years dated from 605, 597, or 586 B.C.—the years of the three significant deportations).

Although Daniel probably knew his advanced age would prevent his return to the land of Judah, we can be sure his heart's desire was for the restoration of his people to their homeland. Because he understood that would soon be coming to pass, we see him in Daniel 9 turning to God in prayer, asking Him to fulfill His Word and restore the Jewish people.

God's response to Daniel in verses 20-27 was a major revelation of the future. It was not the first prophecy given to Daniel: Daniel 2 records a prophecy of four great Gentile empires succeeded by the kingdom of God (vv. 19-45). Daniel 7 records the same vision in a different format, which includes the reign of the Antichrist over the final form of the last Gentile world power (vv. 1-28).

From Daniel 8 on the focus of the book turns from the future of the Gentile world powers to the future of Israel. We can see that in the prophecy given to Daniel in chapter 9: "Seventy weeks are determined upon *thy people* and upon *thy holy city*" (v. 24, emphasis added).

# Lesson

## I. THE PRAYER PRECEDING THE REVELATION (v. 20)

"[An answer to my prayer came] while I was speaking, and praying, and confessing my sin and the sin of my people, Israel, and presenting my supplication before the Lord, my God, for the holy mountain of my God."

### A. Daniel's Commitment to Prayer

Daniel was a man of prayer—verse 20 shows him doing what it was his habit to do. He did not approach God in a superficial fashion: verse 3 records that he came with supplication, fasting, sackcloth, and ashes. His custom was to face Jerusalem and pray three times each day (Dan. 6:10). He was so committed to prayer that it was used as a weapon against him by his enemies and he was thrown into a lions' den (Dan. 6:1-18). Yet God honored his commitment and sustained him for his faithfulness.

### B. Daniel's Method of Prayer

Verse 20 tells us that Daniel's prayer consisted of "speaking," "praying," "confessing," and "presenting . . . supplication." We find each of those verbs in verses 3-19. That was the Holy Spirit's way of summarizing Daniel's prayer and indicating it was in the midst of that prayer that God's answer arrived.

Daniel's prayer had the proper focus (James 4:3). Most people pray selfishly, seeking only to satisfy their own desires. But Daniel prayed for the sake of "the holy mountain of [his] God" (v. 20)—for Zion, which figuratively represents the glory of God. It grieves me when I hear people say we are to demand things from God and claim what belongs to us. Daniel prayed for God's glory and was rewarded with understanding from God.

As I studied Daniel's prayer I was led to consider my own prayer life. I wondered at the power of such prayer and the reward it brought Daniel. If we were to follow the characteristics of Daniel's prayer, we might be blessed by God with a portion of what Daniel received.

There are a number of characteristics that made Daniel's prayer answerable.

1. It was in response to God's Word

   The prayer begins, "I, Daniel, understood by books the number of the years, concerning which the word of the Lord came to Jeremiah, the prophet, that he would accomplish seventy years in the desolations of Jerusalem. And I set my face unto the Lord God, to seek [Him] by prayer" (vv. 2-3). Daniel apparently read Jeremiah 25-29, which speaks of the seventy-year exile of God's people in Babylon. He understood God's purposes according to His Word and that's what framed the contents of his prayer. The contents of our prayers are to be similar in nature.

2. It was according to God's will

   Daniel prayed that God would perform His revealed will. Verses 3-18 form a long preparation for the only request we find in Daniel's prayer: "O Lord, hear; O Lord, forgive; O Lord, hearken and *do*" (v. 19; emphasis added). The apostle John said, "If we ask any thing according to his will, he heareth us; and if we know that he hear us, whatever we ask, we know that we have the petitions that we desired of him" (1 John 5:14-15; cf. John 14:14). Confidence in prayer requires that we pray in accord with God's will.

3. It was fervent

   The phrase "I set my face" in verse 3 is a Hebraism for a resolute and fervent spirit. He prayed with fasting, and sackcloth, and ashes (v. 3). Some commentators think the angel Gabriel began flying toward Daniel with God's answer when Daniel began to fast (v. 23)—God knew and answered

Daniel's request even before he uttered it because of the attitude he displayed.

4. It included self-denial

As part of his prayer Daniel "made [his] confession." He recognized he was unworthy to enter the presence of God. That's to be our attitude also.

5. It focused on others

In verses 5-11 Daniel makes extensive use of the first person plural. Daniel's prayer was not selfish but a prayer for his people.

6. It included corporate confession of sin

In his prayer Daniel identified with the sins of his people: "We have sinned, and have committed iniquity, and have done wickedly, and have rebelled, even by departing from thy precepts and from thine ordinances; neither have we hearkened unto thy servants, the prophets" (vv. 5-6).

7. It presupposed dependence on God

In verse 4 Daniel describes God as "the great and awesome God, keeping the covenant and mercy to them that love him, and to them that keep his commandments." He recognized that all answers to prayer depend on the absolute and unchanging promises of an unchanging God.

8. It glorified God

The ultimate purpose of Daniel's prayer was the glory of God. He said to the Lord that Israel should be restored "for thine own sake, . . . for thy city and thy people are called by thy name" (v. 19).

In verse 21 Daniel says that the angel Gabriel came and touched him "about the time of the evening oblation." Daniel prayed to God at the special time of day when the

13

evening sacrifice and prayers were offered in the Temple at Jerusalem (cf. Ezra 9:4-5).

Daniel would have remembered that time from his childhood in Jerusalem. A lamb would be brought, and the one who brought it would place his hands on it to signify identification with the lamb that symbolically bore his sin. Smoke would rise in the evening sky as the lamb was then slain and offered as a sacrifice for sin. Meal and drink offerings were also made at that time.

No sacrifices had been offered in the Temple since 586 B.C. Doubtless many who were taken into captivity with Daniel forgot them. But Daniel remembered and found it a fitting time to confess his sins, making it a part of his tradition of turning to God in prayer every day.

II. THE MESSENGER OF THE REVELATION (vv. 21-23)

"While I was speaking in prayer, even the man, Gabriel, whom I had seen in the vision at the beginning, being caused to fly swiftly, touched me about the time of the evening oblation. And he informed me, and talked with me, and said, O Daniel, I am now come forth to give thee skill and understanding. At the beginning of thy supplications, the commandment came forth, and I am come to show thee; for thou art greatly beloved. Therefore, understand the matter, and consider the vision."

A. Who He Was

While Daniel prayed Gabriel arrived—testimony to the speed of an angelic being. There's no doubt Gabriel is an angel though he is described as "even the man, Gabriel" (v. 21). That identifies him as the same Gabriel who appeared to Daniel in human form in Daniel 8:16.

The Hebrew word *ish*, which describes Gabriel as a man, can also be translated "servant." Gabriel was a man in the sense that he acted as God's servant.

Apparently Gabriel appeared in human form the second time so that Daniel would be able to recognize God's

14

messenger. Gabriel is a supreme messenger angel sent only with messages of importance. If he appeared as a spirit it's possible Daniel wouldn't have recognized him or ascertained the importance God placed on the delivery of His message.

The last two letters of Gabriel's name signify one of the names of God (Heb., *el*, "the strong one"). The first part of Gabriel's name is derived from the Hebrew word *gabor*, which also means "the strong one," but in reference to man. Thus the compound meaning of Gabriel's name is "man, the strong one; God, the strong one" or "the strong man of God."

## B. The Message He Brought

Daniel's praying was so intense—his eyes were probably closed and his head bowed—that it was necessary for Gabriel to alert him of his arrival by touching him. Daniel was not praying for understanding, yet Daniel 9:22 says that Gabriel brought him a message to impart "skill and understanding"—two words that mean virtually the same thing. Nor did Daniel request something for himself or insight into the future. Daniel was concerned with God's plan for His people Israel, and Gabriel was sent to assure Daniel of God's unwavering purpose to fulfill His promises.

## C. The Time He Came

As we already noted, some commentators believe Gabriel was sent to Daniel before he began to pray because in verse 23 Gabriel says, "At the beginning of thy supplications, the commandment came forth, and I am come to show thee." Daniel's supplications began with a period of fasting (v. 3) before audible prayer. It was at the beginning of Daniel's process of prayer that the command for an answer to be delivered by Gabriel was issued from the throne of God—the source of all commands given to angels.

## D. The Love He Expressed

Gabriel gave Daniel a reason for his being sent with an answer: "Thou art greatly beloved" (v. 23). John, in his gospel, mentioned the other apostles by name, but described himself as the disciple whom Jesus loved (John 21:20). He understood that being known as one beloved by God was far better than being known by one's own name. We too ought to rejoice in being known as God's beloved.

That doesn't mean God loves some more than others. His love is so unrestricted that He gave His only begotten Son for the entire world (John 3:16). Jesus said, "Greater love hath no man than this, that a man lay down his life for his friends" (John 15:13). So great a love isn't measured out in degrees. But from a human perspective God's love is experienced to the utmost when one's character is what it ought to be. A godly man or woman will experience God's love more fully than others, and Daniel was a godly man.

Jude 20-21 says, "Ye, beloved, building up yourselves on your most holy faith, praying in the Holy Spirit, keep yourselves in the love of God." We know from other Scriptures that Jude didn't mean a Christian can step outside of God's love in an ultimate sense. Rather he was saying that by obedience we maintain the enjoyment of God's love and blessing. To be disobedient is to step outside the sphere of God's love and blessing.

Although God didn't love Daniel more than others, Daniel's obedience to the will of God put him in a greater position than most to receive His blessing. Many, because of their ungodly character, are in no such position. But Daniel was in the center of God's will and therefore able to receive the showers of blessing God desires to rain on all. We ought to desire a character like Daniel's that, for one thing, we might receive the blessings he received.

The blessing God poured out on Daniel through Gabriel was revelation. In verse 23 Gabriel tells Daniel that he was to "understand the matter, and consider the vision." The Hebrew word translated "vision" speaks of an appearance. Daniel didn't receive a vision but the actual appearance of an angelic messenger.

III. THE CONTENT OF THE REVELATION (vv. 24-27)

"Seventy weeks are determined upon thy people and upon thy holy city, to finish the transgression, and to make an end of sins, and to make reconciliation for iniquity, and to bring in everlasting righteousness, and to seal up the vision and prophecy, and to anoint the most Holy. Know, therefore, and understand, that from the going forth of the commandment to restore and to build Jerusalem unto the Messiah, the Prince, shall be seven weeks, and threescore and two weeks; the street shall be built again, and the wall, even in troublous times. And after threescore and two weeks shall Messiah be cut off, but not for himself; and the people of the prince that shall come shall destroy the city and the sanctuary, and the end of it shall be with a flood, and unto the end of the war desolations are determined. And he shall confirm the covenant with many for one week; and in the midst of the week he shall cause the sacrifice and the oblation to cease, and for the overspreading of abominations he shall make it desolate, even until the consummation, and that determined shall be poured upon the desolate."

That prophecy deals with the nation of Israel and the city of Jerusalem. There are two princes mentioned: the Messiah (who is Christ, v. 25) and another who will come (the Antichrist, v. 26). The time period covered by the prophecy is seventy weeks, divided into three periods: seven weeks, sixty-two weeks, and one week. The time period began "from the going forth of the commandment to restore and build Jerusalem" (v. 25) and will end when Messiah the Prince comes to establish His eternal kingdom.

Verse 24 says, "Seventy weeks are determined upon thy people." *Determined* tells us God is in control of history and has predetermined its events. The Hebrew word literally means "to cut off." God has cut off a segment of time and assigned it for the deliverance of His people Israel and the

17

city of Jerusalem. Daniel had prayed for both, and God's answer encompassed all Daniel asked for.

## A. God's Purpose in History (v. 24)

Verse 24 outlines six purposes that God will accomplish for Israel and Jerusalem. Three are negative and three are positive.

### 1. Stated in a negative sense

#### a) "To finish the transgression"

That literally means "to restrain firmly the transgression." Today sin expresses itself freely, but a day will come when that will not be true. Jesus will rule with a rod of iron (Ps. 2:6-9) and every expression of evil—"transgression"—will be immediately restrained by His divine power.

#### b) "To make an end of sins"

That means sin will be done away with in general and individually (the plural denotes that individual sins will be dealt with). Some think the Hebrew verb translated "to make an end" might be better translated "to seal up." It's a word always associated with divine judgment. The idea is that at the end of the seventy weeks God will wipe out sin.

#### c) "To make reconciliation for iniquity"

"To make reconciliation" translates the Hebrew verb *kaphar*, which means "to cover." It speaks of expiation and atonement. This tells us how God will put an end to transgression and sin: by atoning for it. That was surely a welcome word to Daniel because it was sin that caused Israel to be taken into captivity.

What Daniel may not have understood was that was speaking of the coming of Christ and His work on the cross. That's where sin was dealt with, though the full effect of that work will be fully realized only when Christ comes again. Thus the first three negative purposes spoken of in verses 24-27 pertain to the cross and its provision for sin.

2. Stated in a positive sense

a) "To bring in everlasting righteousness"

"Righteousness" is stated as a plural in the Hebrew text and refers to an everlasting era of righteousness. The Jewish people didn't distinguish in the Old Testament between the Messiah's first and second coming, nor did they understand the gap that exists between them—the church age, which is called a "mystery" in the New Testament (cf. Eph. 3:2-6). We see a hint of that time in the transition between this fourth purpose of God and the three that precede it: the first three deal with the work of Christ on the cross (at the end of Daniel's sixty-ninth week), whereas this and the following two represent Christ establishing His eternal kingdom of righteousness (at the end of the seventieth week).

b) "To seal up the vision and prophecy"

When the eternal kingdom of Christ is established, there will be no need for vision or prophecy. Some think "to seal up the vision and prophecy" speaks of the completion of the New Testament. But that can't be true because Joel 2:28-29 indicates that prophecy and visions will occur at the initiation of the kingdom, which is yet future. Therefore, though an exact chronology is not specified, what is spoken of here is the end of prophecies and visions at the inauguration of Christ's kingdom.

c) "To anoint the Most Holy"

The phrase "the Most Holy" occurs thirty-nine times in the Old Testament and always has some reference to the Holy of Holies in the Tabernacle and Temple. It always refers to a place, indicating that when Christ's kingdom is inaugurated, there will be a Temple: the restored Temple of the millennial kingdom (cf. Ezek. 40-48).

## Conclusion

The prophecy of Daniel 9:24-27 stretches from Daniel's day to the reign of the Messiah on earth. During that time sin would be atoned for (the work of Christ on the cross), and at its end the kingdom of Christ will be inaugurated. Between those two events (the sixty-ninth and seventieth week) is a gap of unspecified duration. That's an important period of history for us—we're in it now!

## Focusing on the Facts

1. How did Daniel come to be in Babylon? Why was he selected as prime minister in both the Babylonian and Medo-Persian empires (see p. 9)?
2. When the prophecy of Daniel 9 was given, how long had Judah been captive (see p. 9)?
3. What was the cause of Daniel's prayer in Daniel 9 (Dan. 9:2; see p. 10).
4. What's the focus of the book of Daniel from chapter 8 on? Support your answer with Scripture (see p. 10).
5. Describe Daniel's commitment to prayer (see p. 11).
6. Compare the focus of most people in prayer and that of Daniel: how do they differ (see p. 11)?
7. Daniel understood God's purposes according to His _____ _____ and that's what framed the contents of his _____ _____ (see p. 12).
8. What does "I set my face" (Dan 9:3) tell us about Daniel's attitude (Dan 9:3; see p. 12)?
9. Daniel's prayer was not selfish but a prayer for _____ _____ (see p. 13).

10. What did Daniel recognize that all answers to prayer depend on (see p. 13)?

11. In what form did the angel Gabriel appear to Daniel? Why (see pp. 14-15).

12. Does the phrase "thou art greatly beloved" (Dan. 9:23) mean that God loves some more than others? Why or why not (see p. 16)?

13. What did Daniel's obedience to the will of God put him in a greater position than most to receive (see p. 16)?

14. In the seventy weeks mentioned in Daniel 9:24 God has cut off a segment of time and assigned it for what (see p. 18)?

15. How will every expression of evil be immediately restrained by divine power in the future (Ps. 2:6-9; see p. 18)?

16. What do the first three negative purposes spoken of in Daniel 9:24-27 pertain to (see p. 19)?

17. What distinction in the Old Testament did the Jewish people not see (see p. 19)?

18. Why is the gap that occurs between the sixty-ninth and seventieth week of Daniel important? What is it called in the New Testament (Eph. 3:2-6; see pp. 19)?

## Pondering the Principles

1. Prayer is the mark of a Christian. How often do you communicate with God through Christ? Christians are to be a prayerful people and the key to prayer can be summed up in two words: Do it! Make time for prayer and then pray. Although you may not receive an immediate answer—or the one you expect—keep praying. God will reward your faithfulness just as He rewarded Daniel. Once prayer is your habit, look for God's answers and respond with gratitude.

2. The six purposes that God will accomplish for Israel and Jerusalem (Dan. 9:24-27; see pp. 17-20) can be reduced to one negative and one positive. God has dealt with man's greatest negative: sin. And He has provided men and women with a great positive: righteousness. That those are His eternal purposes can be seen from reading Ephesians 1. Consider how you might share those two purposes of

God with an unsaved person. They may serve as an apt response in a conversation about world problems.

# 2
## Israel's Future—Part 2

**Outline**

Introduction

Review
I.   The Prayer Preceding the Revelation (v. 20)
II.  The Messenger of the Revelation (vv. 21-23)
III. The Content of the Revelation (vv. 24-27)
A. God's Purpose in History (v. 24)

Lesson
B. God's Timing in History (vv. 24-25)
    1. Defining the terms
        *a*) "Weeks"
            (1) According to immediate context
            (2) According to a familiar concept
            (3) According to extended context
            (4) According to prophetic reckoning
        *b*) "Year"
            (1) According to the Flood record
            (2) According to Tribulation prophecy
    2. Determining the Messiah's arrival
        *a*) The first seven weeks
            (1) When they commence
                (*a*) At the decree of Cyrus?
                (*b*) At the decree of Artaxerxes?
                (*c*) At the second decree of Artaxerxes?

23

## Introduction

The prophet Jeremiah is known as the weeping prophet. He lived before the people of Judah went into captivity and his ministry was to warn them of coming judgment by God. The Jewish people cherished their national identity and independence, as well as their identification as God's chosen people. As a result Jeremiah's message was not well received—though he warned them for years, he was ignored, shoved aside, and finally thrown into a pit (Jer. 38:1-6).

Jeremiah lived to see his prophecies of destruction fulfilled. He watched the siege and capture of Jerusalem by the Babylonians and saw his people taken captive. Jeremiah wrote of that captivity, and his prophecies concerning its duration provide a meaningful setting for the ninth chapter of Daniel: "Behold, I will send and take all the families of the north, saith the Lord, and [Nebuchadnezzar], the king of Babylon, my servant, and will bring them against this land, and against its inhabitants, and against all these nations round about, and will utterly destroy them, and make them an horror, and an hissing, and perpetual desolations. Moreover, I will take from them the voice of mirth, and the voice of gladness, the voice of the bridegroom, and the voice of the bride, the sound of the millstones, and the light of the lamp. And this whole land shall be a desolation, and an horror; and these nations shall serve the king of Babylon seventy years" (Jer. 25:9-11).

That very prophecy may be what caused Daniel to pray as he did in Daniel 9 since he says in verse 2, "In the first year of [Darius's] reign I, Daniel, understood by books the number of the years, concerning which the word of the Lord came to Jeremiah, the prophet, that he would accomplish seventy years in the desolations

24

of Jerusalem." Daniel was led to pray not because he had just discovered Jeremiah's prophecy but because he had been in captivity for almost seventy years. He was probably also aware that Isaiah prophesied that Cyrus (the proper name of the man identified by the title Darius in Dan. 9:1) would decree a return of the Jewish people to their homeland (Isa. 44:28). Jeremiah prophesied that the restoration of Israel would be preceded by spiritual renewal (Jer. 29:10-14), so Daniel turned "unto the Lord God, to seek by prayer and supplications, with fasting, and sackcloth, and ashes" (Dan. 9:3), confessing his sin and the sins of his people.

Like Daniel, we also study prophecy to understand God's purposes in history. And Daniel 9 is a good perspective on how to understand and apply prophecy.

### Review

I. THE PRAYER PRECEDING THE REVELATION (v. 20; see pp. 11-14)

II. THE MESSENGER OF THE REVELATION (vv. 21-23; see pp. 14-17)

III. THE CONTENT OF THE REVELATION (vv. 24-27; see pp. 17-20)
A. God's Purpose in History (v. 24; see pp. 18-20)

### Lesson

B. God's Timing in History (vv. 24-25)

"Seventy weeks are determined upon thy people and upon thy holy city, to finish the transgression, and to make an end of sins, and to make reconciliation for iniquity, and to bring in everlasting righteousness, and to seal up the vision and prophecy, and to anoint the most Holy. Know, therefore, and understand, that from the going forth of the commandment to restore and to build Jerusalem unto the Messiah, the Prince, shall be seven weeks, and threescore and two weeks; the street shall be built again, and the wall, even in troublous times."

The key to understanding God's purpose in history is in determining God's timing in history—in this case the duration of the seventy weeks mentioned here.

1. Defining the terms

   a) "Weeks"

      The Hebrew word translated "weeks" (*shabuwa*), literally means "sevens." The word doesn't by itself indicate whether it is speaking of days, weeks, months, or years, so it must be interpreted in its context. In Daniel 9, I think it refers to weeks of years, as do many evangelical Bible scholars. There are a number of reasons for interpreting *shabuwa* that way.

      (1) According to immediate context

         Daniel was already thinking in sevens of years. By reading Jeremiah's prophecy he may have thought that all God's purposes would be accomplished in seventy years. But in a possible play on words, God is telling him in verse 24 that His purposes would not be accomplished in seventy years, but in seven times seventy years. Restoration to the land would occur at the end of Jeremiah's seventy years, but there was more to come in God's plans for Israel.

      (2) According to a familiar concept

         The concept of weeks of years was familiar to the Jewish people. The land was to have a rest from farming every seven years and the poor were to be allowed to take whatever it produced (Lev. 25:3-4). After seven weeks of seven years (a total of forty-nine years) came a time known as the year of jubilee (vv. 8-10). In that year the land was to rest, all estates were to be returned to their original owners, all debts forgiven, and slaves freed (vv. 11-13, 39-43).

(3) According to extended context

The only other time Daniel used the term *shabuwa* was in Daniel 10:2-3. In both verses Daniel refers to three whole or full weeks, with the important addition in the Hebrew text where he added the word "days" (unlike the Hebrew text of Dan. 9:24). It's as though Daniel was helping his readers to distinguish between the weeks of years in Daniel 9:24 and weeks of days in Daniel 10:2-3.

(4) According to prophetic reckoning

Daniel knew one of the reasons the Jewish people were taken into captivity was their constant violation of the seven-year Sabbath. Instead of allowing the land a year of rest, their greed and materialism caused them to plow and plant the seventh year. That violation was repeated over an extended period of time, and God determined that the land belonging to Him would have its rest.

The Jewish people were taken captive "to fulfill the word of the Lord by the mouth of Jeremiah, until the land had enjoyed her sabbaths; for as long as she lay desolate she kept sabbath, to fulfill threescore and ten years" (2 Chron. 36:21). They had violated seventy sabbath years, which means they had disobeyed the sabbath commandment for 490 of their 800-year history as a nation. God exacted one year of captivity for each sabbath year violated.

*b)* "Year"

In Daniel's day some used 365-day years and others 360-day years. Those who used 360-day years would occasionally add an extra month to catch up. There are two compelling reasons to believe the years of Daniel 9 are 360-day years.

(1)   According to the Flood record

According to Genesis 7:11 and 8:4 the Flood began on the seventeenth day of the second month and ended on the seventeenth day of the seventh month (a total of five months). According to Genesis 7:24 and 8:3 the Flood lasted 150 days. That indicates the Jewish people were using months of thirty days, of which twelve made a year of 360 days.

(2)   According to Tribulation prophecy

Daniel 7:25 indicates that the Great Tribulation (the last half of the seven-year Tribulation) will last "a time, times and half a time" (*New International Version*), or three and a half years. "Time" equals one year. Revelation 13:5 says that the same period will last forty-two months, while Revelation 12:6 says that period will last 1,260 days. A comparison of the three time frames indicates usage of thirty-day months: three-and-a-half years equals forty-two thirty-day months, just as 1,260 equals forty-two thirty-day months.

An examination of the Bible from Genesis to Revelation indicates usage of thirty-day months. Thus the time period indicated in Daniel 9:24 is a period of 490 years (seventy weeks of years) of 360 days each.

2.   Determining the Messiah's arrival

Daniel 9:25 says, "[The time] unto the Messiah, the Prince, shall be seven weeks, and threescore and two weeks; the street shall be built again, and the wall, even in troublous times." The sixty-nine weeks leading to the coming of the Messiah are divided into two time periods of seven and sixty-two weeks. Verse 27 indicates that the seventieth week is separated from the other sixty-nine, so only 483 years of the total 490 involved in Daniel's prophecy span the time between the command concerning Jerusalem and the coming of the Messiah. That is the time period we will consider here.

*a*)  The first seven weeks

   (1)  When they commence

      Verse 25 indicates that they begin with "the commandment to restore and build Jerusalem"—but history records several such commands given on different dates. It's important to know which one is right since a different starting date would result in a different ending date. Bible scholars have suggested three possibilities.

      (*a*)  At the decree of Cyrus?

         Ezra 1:1-4 records a decree made by Cyrus in 536 B.C. Some scholars think that must be the decree mentioned in Daniel's prophecy because God said of Cyrus through Isaiah, "He is my shepherd, and shall perform all my pleasure; even saying to Jerusalem, Thou shalt be built; and to the temple, Thy foundation shall be laid" (Isa. 44:28). But 483 years subtracted from 536 B.C. takes us to 53 B.C., many years before the birth of Christ and still more from the inception of His ministry—a discrepancy of more than eighty years.

Over the span of hundreds of years eighty years or so may seem close, but our God isn't close—He's exact! Some have proposed a revision of the Ptolemaic calendar (commonly used before the time of Copernicus) to account for the discrepancy, but that seems an inadequate solution because we can't prove a discrepancy. Also, the actual decree of Cyrus provided only for building the Temple in Jerusalem—not for rebuilding Jerusalem's walls (a necessary part of restoring the city). Thus Cyrus's decree is an unlikely candidate for the command of Daniel 9:25.

(b) At the first decree of Artaxerxes?

The first decree of Artaxerxes in 458 B.C. (Ezra 7:11-26) is considered a possibility. However, 483 years from 458 B.C. takes us to A.D. 26. But the only event of significance in the life of Christ remotely close to A.D. 26 is His baptism. However that wasn't His presentation to the nation as the Messiah, but to the Father for approval. It was a transaction between the Son and the Father, and there's no indication that the people at large understood what happened at Jesus' baptism (Matt. 3:13-17). Also, the first decree of Artaxerxes did not provide for the rebuilding of Jerusalem.

(c) At the second decree of Artaxerxes?

This is the best candidate for the decree spoken of in Daniel 9:25. Two scholars have convincingly researched this view: Sir Robert Anderson of Scotland Yard, who over a hundred years ago wrote the classic book *The Coming Prince* (Grand Rapids: Kregel, 1954), and Harold Hoehner of Dallas Theological Seminary, who wrote *Chronological Aspects of the Life of Christ* (Grand Rapids: Zondervan, 1977). Dr. Hoehner confirmed Anderson's precise computations, differing with him only concerning the proper year of Artaxerxes's accession to his throne.

Ezra 4 records that the restoration of the Temple was temporarily suspended because the builders were accused of rebuilding the city without authorization. Permission for rebuilding the city came only with the second decree of Artaxerxes "in the month Nisan, in the twentieth year of Artaxerxes" (Neh. 2:1). History records that Artaxerxes's reign literally started in 465 B.C., so Sir Robert Anderson concluded the date referred to in Nehemiah 2:1 was the month of Nisan in the year 445 B.C. Because a king's reign was dated from the first of the month of his reign, Anderson thought that since no other date was mentioned in Nehemiah 2, the date Nehemiah spoke of was probably the first of Nisan, 445 B.C.—or March 14, 445 B.C. according, to our calendar.

During the seven weeks indicated in Daniel 9:25 the city of Jerusalem would be rebuilt "even in troublous times." The books of Ezra and Nehemiah reveal that's precisely what happened (Ezra 9 and 10; Neh. 4, 6, 9, and 13). Yet during that forty-nine-year period crucial events occurred in the history of Israel: the city was rebuilt, the Temple established, and the canon of the Old Testament was completed. From the close of that time to the advent of John the Baptist there was no prophet in Israel.

The prophecy that the street and wall of Jerusalem would be rebuilt is best understood to refer to its internal structures and external fortifications (the Hebrew words used literally refer to the marketplace and surrounding moat of the city). The prophecy required that the complete restoration of Jerusalem to take place in forty-nine years. Since history records it was during the half century after the second decree of Artaxerxes that Jerusalem was rebuilt and completed, it seems that decree must be the one that started the seventy weeks prophesied in Daniel 9:24-27.

(2) When they conclude

The seven weeks of years concluded in 396 B.C., forty-nine years after the second decree of Artaxerxes in 445 B.C.

b) The sixty-two weeks

(1) When they commence

In 396 B.C., following the forty-nine years of rebuilding Jerusalem, a period of sixty-two weeks of years (434 years) commenced. Simple addition shows that the total number of years between the second decree of Artaxerxes and the coming of the Messiah is 483 years. Each of those years consisted of 360 days. Thus the total number of days involved is 173,880 days.

(2) When they conclude

The phrase "the Messiah, the Prince" (Heb., *mashiach nagid*) is formal terminology that means "the Anointed One, the Ruler." The Hebrew word translated "prince" (*nagid*) was first used of King Saul and then of other kings. It is a title associated with kingly authority and is applied here to the appearing of the Lord Jesus Christ as a prince and ruler.

But what particular event in Christ's life marks the end of the sixty-two weeks? Two popular views are His baptism and triumphal entry into Jerusalem.

(a) At Christ's baptism?

Some think the appearance spoken of in Daniel 9:25 refers to His baptism. But as we already discussed, that appearance was a presentation to the Father. Those present were unaware of what was occurring, and the Father's declaration was, "This is my beloved Son, in whom I am well pleased" (Matt. 3:17)—not a declaration of Christ's kingly authority.

(b) At Christ's triumphal entry?

The interpretation that makes the most sense is the triumphal entry of Jesus into Jerusalem since that was when He was presented to the Jewish people as the messianic Prince. The test of this theory is whether the triumphal entry occurred 173,880 days after the second decree of Artaxerxes.

Working from March 14, 445 B.C. (the date of Artaxerxes's second decree according to our calendar; see p. 31), Sir Robert Anderson calculated by the use of astronomical calendars and charts that the day of the Messiah's coming was April 6, A.D. 32. Such calendars and charts helped him determine the timing of the Jewish new moons by which the Passovers were determined.

One of the problems Anderson had to resolve in his calculations was that between the decree of Artaxerxes and the triumphal entry of Jesus into Jerusalem there appeared to be a period of 477 years and 24 days, not 483 years (sixty-nine prophetic weeks). After deducting one year to account for the fact that 1 B.C. and A.D. 1 are not two years but one, that left Anderson with a total of 476 years and 24 days or a total of 173,764 days—not the necessary 173,880 days. That's close—but our God is precise!

Anderson next added 119 days to his figure for the 119 leap years represented by 476 years. That results in a figure of 173,883 days—three days too many! But realizing that the Julian calendar on which our 365-day year is based is slightly inaccurate compared to an actual solar year, Anderson checked with the Royal Observatory in London and found that a 365-day year exceeds a solar year by 1/128th of a day. That fraction of 476 years is three days, which when subtracted from 173,883 yields a difference of 173,880 days—precisely the number of days predicted in Daniel 9:25!

More recently Harold Hoehner used modern astronomical charts and computers to confirm the work of Sir Robert Anderson. However, he used a different starting date than Anderson. That's because he knew that Medo-Persian kings didn't include the year of their accession to the throne to reckon the length of their reigns. That meant Artaxerxes wasn't considered king until 464 B.C., and thus rather than using 445 B.C. as the year of Artaxerxes's second decree (as Anderson did), Hoehner used 444 B.C. (twenty years after Artaxerxes was first recognized as king—Neh. 2:1). It also meant that the first of Nisan fell on March 30 (according to the new moons of 444 B.C.) rather than March 5.

Using the same adjustments as Anderson, Hoehner multiplied 476 (the number of solar years between the second decree of Artaxerxes and the presentation of the Messiah in Jerusalem) by 365.24219879 (the decimal equivalent of 365 days, five hours, forty-eight minutes, and forty-four seconds—which accounts for the 1/128 difference between calendar and solar days observed by Anderson) and obtained a product of 173,855.28662404 days (173,855 days, six hours, fifty-two minutes, and forty-four seconds). That's twenty-five days longer than the 173,880 that ought to exist from the time of the decree to the time of the Messiah's appearance. But Hoehner was able to adjust that amount by the difference between the starting dates of Anderson (March 5) and himself (March 30)—a period of exactly twenty-five days! Thus regardless of the starting date used, both Anderson and Hoehner were able to show the precision with which God predicted and fulfilled the presentation of Jesus Christ as Messiah and Ruler.

### Conclusion

When Jesus entered Jerusalem in triumph, it wasn't on a whim. When He said, "Mine hour is not yet come," He knew what He was talking about: God has declared "the end from the beginning, and from ancient times the things that are not yet done" (Isa. 46:10). God told Daniel precisely when the Messiah would enter Jerusalem and be acknowledged as King with shouts of "Hosanna to the Son of David!" (Matt. 21:9).

1. Describe Jeremiah's ministry to the Jewish people. What was his message? How did they respond (see p. 24)?
2. How did Daniel learn of the length of time the Jewish people would be in captivity (see pp. 24-25)?
3. What did Daniel know about the restoration of Israel that prompted him to pray for his people (see p. 25)?
4. What does the Hebrew word for "weeks" (Dan. 9:24) mean? What do the "weeks" in Daniel 9 represent (see pp. 26)?
5. How many days are in a prophetic year? What two biblical events support that (see p. 28)?
6. What command marks the beginning of the "seventy weeks" of Daniel 9:25 (Neh. 2:1; see pp. 30-31)?
7. What is the date of the decree that best corresponds to the rebuilding of Jerusalem? What are the problems with the two early dates (see p. 29-31)?
8. When does history record the rebuilding of Jerusalem took place? Under what conditions was it rebuilt (Dan. 9:25; see p. 32)?
9. What event marked the end of the sixty-two "week" period (see p. 33)?
10. On what date does Harold Hoehner believe the triumphal entry of Christ into Jerusalem took place? Why does he differ by approximately one year from the date used by Robert Anderson (see pp. 34-35)?

## Pondering the Principles

1. Second Chronicles 36:21 says that the captivity of Judah took place "to fulfill the word of the Lord by the mouth of Jeremiah, until the land had enjoyed her sabbaths; for as long as she lay desolate she kept sabbath, to fulfill three-score and ten years." God announced through Jeremiah that Judah would go into captivity for seventy years because for 490 years the nation had violated God's command to give the land its seven-year Sabbath rest. Yet despite Jeremiah's warning, the nation of Judah refused to face the

consequences of its actions. Have you faced the consequences of your present actions on your future? Do your actions glorify God—or yourself? Have you ignored the warnings of Scripture and its promises of blessing to the obedient? Meditate on Galatians 6:7-10 and ask God to direct you in proper obedience to Him.

2. Prophecy is an effective means of demonstrating the accuracy of Scripture. Daniel 9 is a prophecy of amazing accuracy when compared to its clear fulfillment in history. Familiarize yourself with the dates and calculations involved in Daniel's sixty-nine weeks. Ask God to give you an opportunity to share that information with others. It shows the purpose of the life and death of Jesus, and that the God who makes "known the end from the beginning, from ancient times, what is still to come" (Isa. 46:10, NIV) has indeed planned history.

# 3
## Israel's Future—Part 3

### Outline

Introduction
A. God Has Promised Israel a Future
   1. 1 Samuel 12:22
   2. Psalm 89:31-37
   3. Psalm 94:14
   4. Romans 11:1
   5. Luke 21:24
B. God Has Planned Israel's Preservation

Review
  I. The Prayer Preceding the Revelation (v. 20)
 II. The Messenger of the Revelation (vv. 21-23)
III. The Content of the Revelation (vv. 24-25)
   A. God's Purpose in History (v. 24)
   B. God's Timing in History (vv. 24-25)

Lesson
   C. God's Future for Israel (vv. 26-27)
     1. Their treatment of Christ (v. 26a)
       a) When it occurred
       b) What it entailed
         (1) They rejected His Person
         (2) They denied Him His portion
     2. Their treatment by the people of the Antichrist
       (v. 26b)
       a) The Antichrist identified
       b) The people identified

## Introduction

Israel remains at the center stage of redemptive history. Despite the many issues facing modern society, our focus is constantly drawn to the Middle East and the nation of Israel—a country smaller than the state of New Jersey. Yet despite its importance, when a well-known Bible teacher was asked about the significance of the modern state of Israel not long ago, he replied, "It has utterly no significance at all because God is finished with Israel as of the crucifixion of their Messiah."

The Bible, however, clearly affirms that God is not through with Israel.

### A. God Has Promised Israel a Future

1. 1 Samuel 12:22—"The Lord will not forsake his people for his great name's sake." God will not forsake the Jewish people because His reputation is at stake. He bound Himself to Abraham by an unbreakable covenant (cf. Genesis 15), and He will fulfill it.

2. Psalm 89:31-37—God said of Israel, "If they violate my decrees and fail to keep my commands, I will

40

punish their sin with the rod, their iniquity with flogging; but I will not take my love from [them], nor will I ever betray my faithfulness. I will not violate my covenant or alter what my lips have uttered. Once for all, I have sworn by my holiness—and I will not lie to David—that his line will continue forever and his throne endure before me like the sun; it will be established forever like the moon, the faithful witness in the sky" (NIV).

3. Psalm 94:14—"The Lord will not reject his people; he will never forsake his inheritance" (NIV).

4. Romans 11:1—Paul asked the rhetorical question, "Hath God cast away his people?" His immediate reply was, "God forbid." In the Greek text Paul's answer (*me genoito*) carries the meaning "may it never be!"—the strongest negative declaration found in the New Testament.

5. Luke 21:24—In the Olivet discourse (recorded in Matthew, Mark, and Luke) Jesus predicted that the time of Gentile dominion over the land of Israel—though lasting from the time of Babylon—would indeed end. That reaffirmed God's promise that the Jewish people would be restored to the enjoyment of covenant blessing (cf. Ezek. 36:24-27; Amos 9:11-15).

B. God Has Planned Israel's Preservation

We live at an incredible time in history. The Jewish people have survived the melting pot of history and are regathering in their own land. They have a reason to exist: God's purposes concerning them have been fulfilled for only sixty-nine weeks and there is one week left in God's plan (Dan. 9:24). God's plan for history is being fulfilled in our own time.

I.   PRAYER PRECEDING THE REVELATION (v. 20; see pp. 11-14)

II.  THE MESSENGER OF THE REVELATION (vv. 21-23; see pp. 14-17)

III. THE CONTENT OF THE REVELATION (vv. 24-25; see pp. 17-20)

A. God's Purpose in History (v. 24; see pp. 18-20)

B. God's Timing in History (vv. 24-25; see pp. 25-35)

## Lesson

C. God's Future for Israel (vv. 26-27)

"After threescore and two weeks shall Messiah be cut off, but not for himself; and the people of the prince that shall come shall destroy the city and the sanctuary, and the end of it shall be with a flood, and unto the end of the war desolations are determined. And he shall confirm the covenant with many for one week; and in the midst of the week he shall cause the sacrifice and the oblation to cease, and for the overspreading of abominations he shall make it desolate, even until the consummation, and that determined shall be poured upon the desolate."

1. Their treatment of Christ (v. 26a)

"After threescore and two weeks shall Messiah be cut off, but not for himself."

a) When it occurred

That verse is saying the Messiah would be cut off after sixty-two "weeks." Since that period immediately follows the seven weeks mentioned in Daniel 9:25, this is talking about something that happens after a sixty-nine week period. Christ was crucified shortly after that period of time ended at His triumphal entry into Jerusalem (cf. pp. 33-35).

Since Christ was crucified after the end of the sixty-ninth week, but not during the seventieth week, there must be one week left of the seventy determined for Israel (Dan. 9:24). Verse 27 indicates that is when a coming prince known as the Antichrist "shall confirm the covenant with many." Since that covenant has not yet been declared and nothing occurred in the seven years following Christ's triumphal entry that explains Daniel 9:26-27, there must be a gap between the sixty-ninth and seventieth weeks—they do not occur as a continuous unit of time. Such gaps are common in biblical prophecy.

*b*) What it entailed

(1) They rejected His Person

The Hebrew verb translated "cut off" (*karath*) also means "to kill" or "destroy" (cf. Gen. 9:11; Deut. 20:20; Jer. 11:19). Daniel 9:26 is saying that the Messiah would be killed.

The Jewish people who knew their Bibles should never have concluded that "the preaching of the cross is . . . foolishness" (1 Cor. 1:18). But most of them at the time of Christ didn't understand their Messiah was to be executed, so the cross became "a stumbling block" (v. 23). Jesus had to reprimand His own disciples for their ignorance and explain what Scripture said on the matter (Luke 24:13-27).

*Karath* is used a number of times in the Old Testament to describe the execution of a

43

criminal (Lev. 7:20; Ps. 37:9; Prov. 2:22). Daniel's usage of the term implies the Messiah would die a criminal's death—a prophecy so specific, it seems incomprehensible that when Jesus was presented in triumph in precise accord with Daniel's timetable but then crucified, the Jewish people would not immediately recognize who He was. They waited for centuries for their Messiah to come and then missed Him through hate and despite. And if it is argued that Daniel 9 is somewhat obscure and easily misunderstood, one need only turn to Psalm 22 (which describes the crucifixion in detail) or Isaiah 53 (which describes the suffering and death of the Messiah) to understand that the Old Testament clearly declares the Messiah would die.

(2)  They denied Him His portion

The Messiah was to die, "but not for himself" (Dan. 9:26). That's a hard phrase to interpret, but it apparently means He would die with nothing for Himself. When Jesus died on the cross He received nothing that was due Him: no honor, respect, love, or acceptance. "He was in the world, and the world was made by him, and the world knew him not. He came unto his own, and his own received him not" (John 1:10-11). Instead He received what He didn't deserve: the sins of the world.

2.  Their treatment by the people of the Antichrist (v. 26*b*)

"The people of the prince that shall come shall destroy the city and the sanctuary, and the end of it shall be with a flood, and unto the end of the war desolations are determined."

*a*) The Antichrist identified

"The prince that shall come" is opposite the one identified in Daniel 9:25 as the "Messiah, the Prince." This is the Antichrist (cf. 1 John 2:18, 22; 4:3; 2 John 1:7), who is also called the "little horn" (Dan. 7:8), the "king of fierce countenance" (8:23), the king who does "according to his will" (11:36), and "the man of sin . . . the son of perdition" (2 Thess. 2:3).

*b*) The people identified

The phrase "the people of the prince that shall come" indicates that the Antichrist will be identified with a particular people. The book of Daniel identifies four Gentile world empires that would have a great impact on Israel: Babylon, Medo-Persia, Greece, and Rome (2:31-43; 7:1-8). According to those chapters the Roman Empire will be revived again as a ten-nation confederacy during the last days. Thus the people of the prince to come will have some connection with the Romans and a revived Roman Empire.

*c*) The persecution inflicted

Daniel predicted those people would "destroy the city and the sanctuary" (9:26). In A.D. 70—less than forty years after our Lord was crucified—that prophecy was fulfilled when Jerusalem was destroyed by the Romans. The Antichrist will reign over a revived Roman Empire that will trouble Israel in a way similar to the first Roman Empire.

Daniel predicted that "the end of it shall be with a flood, and unto the end of the war desolations are determined" (9:26). Israel has experienced a steady stream of desolations that began with the destruction of Jerusalem in A.D. 70, but the rise of the Antichrist will commence a holocaust beyond any it has previously experienced. It will be like a flood (cf. Rev. 12:15). That final desolation is vividly prefigured by the first Roman holocaust.

(1)  As foretold by Christ

> Jesus warned, "When ye shall see Jerusalem compassed with armies, then know that its desolation is near. Then let them who are in Judaea flee to the mountains; and let them who are in the midst of it depart; and let not them that are in the countries enter into it. For those are the days of vengeance, that all things which are written may be fulfilled. But woe unto them that are with child, and to them that nurse children, in those days! For there shall be great distress in the land, and wrath upon this people. And they shall fall by the edge of the sword, and shall be led away captive into all nations; and Jerusalem shall be trodden down by the Gentiles, until the times of the Gentiles be fulfilled" (Luke 21:20-24). Jesus' prophecy is focused on the same event Daniel prophesies in Daniel 9:26: the destruction of Jerusalem in A.D. 70.

(2)  As fulfilled in history

> Writing of the Roman conquest of Judea, archeological journalist Werner Keller said, "Old Israel, whose history no longer included the words and works of Jesus, the religious community of Jerusalem, which condemned and crucified Jesus, was extinguished in an inferno which is almost unparalleled in history—the so-called 'Jewish War' of A.D. 66-70" (*The Bible as History* [New York: Bantam Books, 1956], pp. 442-43).

(a) The Jewish revolt

The conflict had its origin in the Jewish people's hatred for the Roman presence in Judea. They hated Jesus because He refused to overthrow the Romans. As time went on, protests against the Romans became more vocal. Groups of zealots and rebels began carrying weapons, and would seek out and slay Roman soldiers at night. Success brought increasing violence and popular support from the Jewish people, and open revolt broke out in May A.D. 66. "The Roman garrison was overrun. Jerusalem fell into the hands of the rebels. The prohibition of the daily sacrifices to the emperor meant an open declaration of war against the Roman world empire. Tiny Jerusalem threw down the gauntlet at Rome's feet and challenged the great Imperium Romanum" (Keller, p. 443).

(b) The Roman conquest

The Roman Emperor Nero gave General Titus Flavius Vespasian, a hero in the Roman conquest of Britain, the task of subduing Israel. With three distinguished Roman legions and other support, he attacked Galilee in the north and subdued that region by October A.D. 67.

Six thousand Jews from Galilee were sent as slaves to build the Corinthian canal. One prisoner was the Jewish general Josephus, who later became a historian and to whom we owe much of our knowledge concerning the conquest of Judea by the Romans. By the spring of A.D. 68 the countryside surrounding Jerusalem had been taken, and all that remained was the taking of Jerusalem itself.

"In the midst of the fighting news came which, for the time being, halted the campaign—Nero had committed suicide. Civil war broke out in Rome. Vespasian awaited developments . . . [and soon] became master of the Roman Empire. From Caesarea on the coast of Palestine where the news reached him, he embarked without delay for Rome, leaving his son Titus to finish the last act of the Jewish War" (Keller, p. 444).

Titus began the final assault on Jerusalem in the spring of A.D. 70. He had clsoe to 100,000 soldiers facing a city with a population of at least 200,000, greatly augmented by a very large number of pilgrims who were present to celebrate the Passover. The city was subjected to artillery that threw massive stones against the walls, and was surrounded by a huge mound to prevent escape. Those who tried to escape or terrorize the enemy were frequently captured and crucified—often 500 were nailed to crosses on a given day. The forests around Jerusalem were completely destroyed to supply the wood necessary for battering rams, ramps, catapults, camp fires, ladders, and the many crosses that rose outside the city.

As time went on, an unbearable stench arose from the bodies of those who had died in battle, from starvation, or on the crosses surrounding Jerusalem. Before the end of the siege thousands of corpses were flung over the city walls by the survivors in Jerusalem. The famine in Jerusalem was severe. Josephus wrote that it "devoured the people by whole houses and families; the upper rooms were full of women and children that were dying by famine, and the lanes of the city were full of the bodies of the aged; the children also and the young men wandered about the market-places like shadows, all swelled with the famine, and fell down dead, wheresoever their misery seized them. As for burying them, those that were sick themselves were not able to do it; and those that were hearty and well were deterred from doing it by the great multitude of those dead bodies, and by the uncertainty there was how soon they should die themselves; for many died as they were burying others" (*Wars of the Jews*, V.xii.3).

Josephus said the misery of the city was incredible: "If so much as the shadow of any kind of food did any where appear, a war was commenced presently, and the dearest friends fell a fighting one with another about it, snatching from each other the most miserable supports of life. Nor would men believe that those who were dying had no food, but the robbers would search them when they were expiring, lest any one should have concealed food in their bosoms, and counterfeited dying; nay, these robbers gaped for want, and ran about stumbling and staggering along like mad dogs, and reeling against the doors of the houses like drunken men; they would also, in the great distress they were in, rush into the very same houses two or three times in one and the same day. Moreover, their hunger was so intolerable, that it obliged them to chew every thing, while they gathered such things as the most sordid animals would not touch, and endured to eat them; nor did they at length abstain from [belts] and shoes; and the very leather which belonged to their shields they pulled off and gnawed: the very wisps of old hay became food to some . . . . But why do I describe the shameless impudence that the famine brought on men in their eating inanimate things, while I am going to relate a matter of fact, the like to which no history relates, either among the Greeks or Barbarians? It is horrible to speak of it, and incredible when heard. I had indeed willingly omitted this calamity of ours, that I might not seem to deliver what is so portentous to posterity, but that I have innumerable witnesses to it in my own age; and besides, my country would have had little reason to thank me for suppressing the miseries that she underwent at this time" (VI.iii.3). Josephus went on to tell what that terrible occurrence was: a mother killed, roasted, and ate her own child because of her hunger!

By August of A.D. 70 the Romans had penetrated the city to the Temple, where they erected their banners and made sacrifices to their gods. Murder and plundering of the city followed. Josephus records that "the number of those that were carried captive during this whole war was collected to be ninety-seven thousand; as was the number of those that perished during the whole siege eleven hundred thousand" (VI.ix.3).

Persecution of the Jewish people continued after the war: in a single day 10,000 Jewish people lost their lives in Damascus. Others died as gladiators in the

Roman games. Daniel prophesied that devastation would come as a flood (Dan. 9:26). Keller concluded that "the inexorable hand of destiny had drawn a line through Israel's part in the concert of nations" (p. 454).

(c) The Roman legacy

The history of the Jews since the Roman holocaust has been one of continual devastation. During the first and second Crusades (attempts by Europeans in 1096 and 1146 to recover Palestine) the Crusaders were afraid that once Palestine was retaken, European Jews would reclaim their ancestral homeland. So during the overland trip to Palestine the Crusaders slaughtered every community of Jews they came across. As a result the Crusades—and Christianity, which is associated with the Crusades—are distasteful reminders of past persecution to Jewish people in our day.

In 1290 Edward I ordered all Jewish people out of England. In France a similar order was issued in 1236, and in one small town three thousand Jewish people were trampled by horses. In 1348-49 (during the time of the Black Death in Europe) Jewish people were accused of poisoning wells and thus causing the outbreak of the bubonic plague. To save themselves many fled to Poland and Russia.

In more modern times the unjust accusations against Captain Alfred Dreyfus, who was Jewish, gave evidence of anti-Semitic bias. In the terrible holocaust inflicted by Hitler prior and during World War II against those he considered undesirables, more than six million Jews perished.

3. Their treatment by the Antichrist (v. 27)

"He shall confirm the covenant with many for one week; and in the midst of the week he shall cause the sacrifice and the oblation to cease, and for the overspreading of abominations he shall make it desolate, even until the consummation, and that determined shall be poured upon the desolate."

The history of the Jewish people is a chronicle of persecution and desolation. Yet it has not ended—in the midst of persecution ninety thousand Jewish people reentered Palestine in 1914. By 1948 Israel was again chartered among the community of nations. This regathering of Israel is in preparation for the final week of Israel's history as declared in Daniel 9, when the Antichrist will come and make a covenant with the nation of Israel.

**Bridging the Gap**

There is a gap between the sixty-ninth and seventieth weeks prophesied in Daniel 9:24-27. During that gap Christ was crucified and the Temple destroyed—a period of approximately forty years. Scripture does not indicate the length of the gap, though we do know it will last until the Antichrist comes to confirm a covenant with Israel (v. 27). Its undetermined length ought not to trouble us: many prophecies in Scripture contain such gaps.

1. Isaiah 9:6—"Unto us a child is born, unto us a son is given, and the government shall be upon His shoulder." While that prophecy speaks both of Christ's birth and future reign on earth, a gap exists between the two.

2. 1 Peter 1:10-11—A great period of time exists between the first and second comings of Christ—a period unperceived by the Old Testament prophets.

3. Luke 4:18-19—In those verses Jesus quoted the portion of Isaiah 61:1-2 that applies to His first advent, but not that

which applies to His return as Judge. He recognized the gap between those two appearances.

4. Ephesians 3:9—That gap is identified as the church age, which Paul called "the mystery, which from the beginning of the ages hath been hidden in God." It's a historical parenthesis within the seventy weeks determined for Israel.

If the seventy weeks of Daniel were 490 consecutive years, there would be no question when our Lord would come again. But because it was intended to be of indeterminate length Jesus said, "Of that day and hour knoweth no man, no, not the angels of heaven, but my Father only" (Matt. 24:36; cf. Acts 1:7).

*a*) He will be welcomed as a hero

The Antichrist will make a treaty with Israel for seven years and will at first be a great hero to them. Even now Israel is looking for support against pressure from the Arab states in the Middle East and continues to fear the potential threat of the Soviet Union to the north.

The only hope for Israel in this situation seems to be a confederated Europe. The United States is too far removed from Israel physically and too mercurial of will to be depended on. A reliable defense for Israel would have to be based on massive power quickly mobilized—the kind represented by a confederated Europe. Daniel predicted that out of that confederation would arise a "little horn," who would be the Antichrist (Dan. 7:8) and make a treaty to protect Israel.

*b*) He will protect Israel for a time

Ezekiel 38 predicts that Israel will feel so secure because of its protection by the Antichrist that her villages will be unwalled—unprepared for war. Armies from the area now occupied by the Soviet Union will descend to conquer Israel (vv. 1-12). But the Antichrist will prove to be a liar and his peace false.

Daniel 9:27 says that "in the midst of the week [the seven-year period] he shall cause the sacrifice and oblation to cease." For that to happen a Temple will have to exist in Jerusalem—the place where sacrifice and oblation would occur. I believe the Antichrist will assist the Jewish people in reestablishing their Temple. Their awe of his willingness and ability to do so may be why they sign a treaty with him.

Revelation 6:2 says the Antichrist will have a bow and will go forth "conquering, and to conquer." He has a bow—but no arrows. That may indicate he will conquer more by statesmanship than force. He will have "a mouth speaking great things" (Dan. 7:8), yet with an intimidating force at his back. He will be able to negotiate the right things for Israel: security, a temple, and the right to worship.

*c*) He will turn against Israel

The middle of the Antichrist's seven-year covenant with Israel marks the beginning of the Great Tribulation. The Antichrist will break the covenant and cause "the overspreading of abominations . . . [and] shall make [the Temple] desolate, even until the consummation, and that determined shall be poured upon the desolate" (Dan. 9:27). That future desolation was previewed in history by the Greek ruler Antiochus Epiphanes, who desecrated the Temple by slaughtering a pig on the altar and forcing the priests to eat pork. That brought on the Maccabean revolt (168-165 B.C.). But that was only a small sample of what the Antichrist will do, for he will bring "the overspreading of abominations."

*d*) He will desecrate the Jewish Temple

Idolatry is an abomination, and Scripture reveals that the Antichrist will desecrate the Temple by setting up an idol of himself there.

(1) Revelation 13:4-15—"They worshiped the dragon [Satan] who gave power unto the beast [the Antichrist]; and they worshiped the beast, saying, Who is like the beast? Who is able to make war with him? And there was given unto him a mouth speaking great things and blasphemies, and power was given unto him to continue forty and two months [the three-and-a-half years of the Great Tribulation]. And he opened his mouth in blasphemy against God, to blaspheme his name, and his tabernacle, and them that dwell in heaven. And it was given unto him to make war with the saints, and to overcome them; and power was given him over all kindreds, and tongues, and nations. And all that dwell on earth shall worship him . . . . And he hath power to give life unto the image of the beast, that the image of the beast should both speak, and cause that as many as would not worship the image of the beast should be killed."

(2) 2 Thessalonians 2:4—The Antichrist will exalt "himself above all that is called God, or that is worshiped, so that he, as God, sitteth in the temple of God, showing himself that he is God."

(3) Revelation 17:16—The Antichrist "shall hate the harlot [the apostate church], and shall make her desolate and naked, and shall eat her flesh, and burn her with fire." The Antichrist will allow the apostate church to exist alongside Israel for the first half of the Tribulation, but at the beginning of the second half he will destroy it and begin persecuting

Israel. Because he will—in Roman fashion—set himself up as a deity, there will be no religion left but the worship of the Antichrist. That will continue "until the consummation, and that determined shall be poured upon the desolate" (Dan. 9:27).

## Conclusion

As bleak a picture as that is, history will not end with the worship of the Antichrist. Daniel 9:24 says that at the end of Israel's seventieth week God will "finish the transgression, and . . . make an end of sins." That includes the destruction of the Antichrist. Then God will "make reconciliation for iniquity, . . . bring in everlasting righteousness, . . . seal up the vision and prophecy, and . . . anoint the most holy" (v. 24). That speaks of the millennial kingdom (Rev. 20:4).

It's an amazing thought that the future history of the world has been hidden "from the wise and prudent, . . . [yet] revealed . . . unto babes" (Matt. 11:25). We ought to be deeply grateful that God has given us the privilege of knowing His plans for the future.

### Focusing on the Facts

1. Show how the Bible affirms that God is not through with Israel (see pp. 40-41).
2. According to Daniel 9:26, what historic event happened after the sixty-ninth week of Daniel 9 (see pp. 42-43)?
3. Why do we understand that there must be a gap between the sixty-ninth and seventieth weeks of Daniel 9 (see p. 43)?
4. What does the Hebrew verb *karath* in Daniel 9:26 tell us would happen to the Messiah (see p. 43)?
5. What couldn't the Jewish people at the time of Christ understand about their Messiah? What did the cross therefore become for many of them (1 Cor. 1:23; see p. 43)?
6. What three Old Testament texts tell us the Messiah would die (see p. 43)?

7. When Jesus died on the cross, what didn't He receive? What did He receive instead (see p. 44)?

8. Identify "the prince that shall come" (Dan. 9:26; see p. 45).

9. What people will "the prince that shall come" (Dan. 9:26) be identified with (see p. 45)?

10. What event do Jesus' prophecy in Luke 21:20-24 and Daniel's prophecy in Daniel 9:26 focus on (see p. 46)?

11. What caused the conflict between the Jews and Romans in A.D. 66-70 (see p. 47)?

12. Describe the course of the Jewish war with the Romans. What hardships did the inhabitants of Jerusalem endure? What was the final result of the war (see pp. 47-51)?

13. Why are the crusades distasteful reminders of past persecution to Jewish people in our day (see pp. 51)?

14. What is the present regathering of Israel in preparation for (see p. 52)?

15. Explain the gap between the sixty-ninth and seventieth weeks prophesied in Daniel 9:24-27. Describe other such gaps reflected in Scripture (see pp. 52-53).

16. What may lead the Jewish people to sign a treaty with the Antichrist (see p. 54)?

17. What historical figure previewed the desolation that will be caused by the Antichrist (see p. 54)?

18. How will the Antichrist desecrate the Temple during the Great Tribulation (see pp. 55-56)?

## Pondering the Principles

1. Psalm 111 recalls God's great works. Verse 9 says, "He provided redemption for his people; he ordained his covenant forever" (NIV). God made a covenant with Israel that can't be broken—and when God says He will do something, He does it! Paul echoes that thought in Romans 8:38-39: "I am convinced that neither death nor life, neither angels nor demons, neither the present nor the future, nor any powers, neither height nor depth, nor anything else in all creation, will be able to separate us from the love of God that is in Christ Jesus" (NIV). Nothing can thwart the promises of God or His faithfulness to them. Take time now to praise God for His sovereign power to fulfill all His promises.

2. God's plan for history is, in a sense, like one of those stories that ends with the familiar phrase "And they lived happily ever after." As terrible as the Tribulation will be, the rebellion of man against God under the Antichrist will be climaxed by "an end of sins" that establishes "everlasting righteousness" (Dan. 9:24). With that kind of outcome, Christians ought to live lives that demonstrate an established hope and trust in God for the future—the kind described in Edward Mote's hymn "The Solid Rock":

My hope is built on nothing less
Than Jesus' blood and righteousness;
I dare not trust the sweetest frame,
But wholly lean on Jesus' name.

How does your life demonstrate what you're hoping for and trusting in?

# 4

# The Vision of Glory

## Outline

Introduction
A. Daniel's Prayer
B. Daniel's Disappointment
C. Daniel's Situation
D. Daniel's Revelation

Lesson
I.   The Mourning of Daniel (vv. 2-3)
    A. The Time of Mourning
    B. The Extent of Mourning
    C. The Reason for Mourning
II.  The Manifestation of Divine Glory (vv. 4-6)
    A. The Place
    B. The Person
       1. His specific identity
          a) Determined from elsewhere in Scripture
          b) Determined from His clothing
       2. His extensive authority
III. The Reaction to the Vision (vv. 7-9)
    A. Of Those with Daniel (v. 7)
       1. Compared to Job
       2. Compared to Isaiah
       3. Compared to Peter
       4. Compared to mankind in the tribulation
    B. Of Daniel Himself (vv. 8-9)
IV.  The Messenger from Heaven (vv. 10-13)
    A. He Revived Daniel

## Introduction

Of the four great revelations recorded in the book of Daniel, the last stretches from Daniel 10 through 12. Chapter 10 introduces the vision, chapter 11 gives the prophecy, and chapter 12 adds an epilogue. Those chapters deal with the same time period as the prophecy of Daniel 8: from Daniel's day to the second coming of Christ. However, Daniel 10-12 gives greater detail about the Tribulation than any other prophecy.

### A. Daniel's Prayer

Daniel 9 records that Daniel had been reading Jeremiah's prophecies and was aware he had prophesied that the captivity of Judah would last seventy years. Daniel realized that those seventy years were nearly over. He therefore began to pray and fast. He confessed his sin and that of his people and asked God to fulfill His promise in allowing the Jewish people to return to their land.

God's answer to Daniel's prayer came in the form of a tremendous prophetic revelation given in the first year of Cyrus, king of the Medo-Persian Empire. In that year Cyrus issued a decree allowing the Jewish people to return home (Ezra 1:1-4). Thus Daniel's prayer was answered in the same year he prayed.

### B. Daniel's Disappointment

Daniel 10 opens "in the third year of Cyrus, king of Persia" (v. 1). That's two years after Daniel received the revelation given in Daniel 9. During that time he experienced terrible discouragement: most of the Jewish people had not returned to their homeland. They were comfortable, paganized, prosperous, and enmeshed in Babylonian society. As a result few cared about the Promised Land, rebuilding Jerusalem, or restoring the Temple.

Of the hundreds of thousands of Jewish people who were in Babylon, a few did return—but only 42,600 (Ezra 2:64). Daniel's desire was that after seventy years of captivity all the Jewish captives would return. He wanted the worship of God reestablished, along with the nation itself. But because so few returned to the land, those goals weren't being accomplished.

C. Daniel's Situation

Two years prior to the vision in Daniel 10, Daniel retired from being one of the prime ministers of the Persian Empire. He had also served in that capacity under the Babylonians. He was about eighty-five years old when he left office in the first year of Cyrus. I believe Daniel didn't return to Judea because of his disappointment that so few returned to the Promised Land. I think he felt responsible to motivate the people to shake off their sinful complacency and return to their country.

D. Daniel's Revelation

Though Daniel would surely have loved to return to his homeland, his burden for his people and the crisis of his disappointment led him to do what he always did in such situations: pray. God's answer came with another revelation: "In the third year of Cyrus, king of Persia, a thing was revealed unto Daniel . . . and the thing was true, but the time appointed was long; and he understood the thing, and had understanding of the vision" (Dan. 10:1).

"The time appointed was long" (*King James Version*) is better translated "one of great conflict" (*New American*

*Standard Bible*). The obscurity of the words *tsavah gadol* in the Hebrew text accounts for the difference. They can also be rendered "a great warfare" or "a great army" (whether of men or angels). Since Daniel 10-12 speaks of great conflict among armies—from holy angels and demons in space, to conflict between Russia and Israel on earth—the context points toward the reading of the *New American Standard Bible*.

## Lesson

I.  THE MOURNING OF DANIEL (vv. 2-3)

"In those days I, Daniel, was mourning three full weeks. I ate no pleasant bread, neither came flesh nor wine in my mouth, neither did I anoint myself at all, till three whole weeks were fulfilled."

A.  The Time of Mourning

Daniel began the account of his vision with the words "I, Daniel," a phrase he used five times to emphasize that the testimony was his. He tells us he mourned for three weeks of days (the Hebrew text specifies that to distinguish them from the weeks of years in Daniel 9). His mourning took place in the third year of Cyrus (v. 1) and ended with an angelic visitation on the twenty-fourth day of the first month (the month of Nisan; v. 4). Since he had been mourning for three weeks, he must have started on the third of Nisan. The Passover always falls on the fourteenth of Nisan, so that means during the festive celebrations of Passover and the feast of Unleavened Bread (the week following Passover) Daniel mourned, prayed, and fasted. Yet for that whole period heaven remained silent.

B.  The Extent of Mourning

During his mourning Daniel "ate no pleasant bread." The Hebrew words mean "bread" or "food of delight." He didn't eat fancy foods, which was one way of fasting—abstinence from certain foods while eating only what was necessary to stay alive. Beyond that "neither came flesh nor wine in [his] mouth" (v. 3). That means he didn't eat normal foods either.

Daniel also refrained from using skin oils during that time. It was customary to anoint one's self with oil for protection from the sun, to keep the skin soft, and to add fragrance to the body. Those privations were a significant undertaking for an eighty-five-year-old man.

C. The Reason for Mourning

At first it may seem strange that Daniel mourned. Only two years previously Cyrus issued a decree allowing the Jewish people to return to their homeland, and 42,600 had returned. Yet that was the problem: though all could return, only a small fraction did. In his selflessness Daniel longed for all his people to return to their land.

II. THE MANIFESTATION OF DIVINE GLORY (vv. 4-6)

"In the four and twentieth day of the first month, as I was by the side of the great river, which is Hiddekel, then I lifted up mine eyes, and looked, and, behold, a certain man clothed in linen, whose loins were girded with fine gold of Uphaz; his body also was like the beryl, and his face like the appearance of lightening, and his eyes like lamps of fire, and his arms and his feet in color like to polished bronze, and the voice of his words like the voice of a multitude."

Daniel's attitude was of the kind God responds to.

A. The Place

"Hiddekel" is the Hebrew name for the Tigris River. It is derived from *idigla*, the ancient Babylonian name for the Tigris. There were two great rivers in ancient Mesopotamia: the Euphrates, on which the city of Babylon was built, and the Tigris, located sixty miles east of Babylon. We don't know why Daniel was at the Tigris—he may have been on official business or he may have gone to encourage a group of Jewish people to return to their homeland.

B. The Person

1. His specific identity

"Behold" in verse 5 expresses the amazement and shock Daniel experienced when confronted by his heavenly visitor. Some think it may have been Gabriel, Michael, or another angel of equal rank. I believe it was a preincarnate appearance of the Second Person of the Trinity—the Lord Jesus Christ (often referred to as a Christophany).

*a*) Determined from elsewhere in Scripture

The description of Daniel's visitor is paralleled in Revelation 1:13-15, where John describes "one like the Son of man, clothed with a garment down to the foot, and girded about the breasts with a golden girdle. His head and his hair were white like wool, as white as snow; and his eyes were like a flame of fire; and his feet like fine bronze, as if they burned in a furnace; and his voice like the sound of many waters." That description is almost identical to Daniel's (except Daniel says nothing of his visitor's hair). John's visitor identified Himself as the "Alpha and Omega" (Rev. 1:8)—the Lord Jesus Christ (vv. 17-18). John saw Christ in His post resurrection glory, Daniel in His preincarnate glory. Jesus Christ was not created when He was born—He existed eternally.

*b*) Determined from His clothing

(1) His garment

Fine white linen was the garment of priests (Ex. 28:39-43) and heavenly visitors such as the angels that appeared at Jesus' tomb (Mark 16:5). It is associated with the representatives of

64

God and seems to symbolize God's foremost attribute: His holiness.

(2)  His belt

The waist of Daniel's visitor was "girded with fine gold of Uphaz" (Dan. 10:5). Although we don't know what Uphaz signifies, Daniel's description indicates a belt overlaid with fine gold. As a valuable, pure, and beautiful metal gold here perhaps symbolizes the sovereignty of God.

(3)  His body

The body of the preincarnate Christ "was like the beryl" (v. 6)—a transparent, flashing jewel called a chrysolite in the Septuagint (the Greek Old Testament). Some think it refers to the topaz. As a flashing, transparent jewel I think it symbolizes God's glory.

(4)  His face

His face was "like the appearance of lightening" (v. 6). In Revelation 1:16 John described Christ's face as being like the sun. That brilliant light brings to mind His omnipotence.

(5)  His eyes

The eyes of Christ were "like lamps of fire" (v. 6). Lamps search out and throw light on what they are aimed at, exposing things as they really are. That pictures God's omniscience.

(6)  His arms and feet

They were "in color like to polished bronze" (v. 6). Bronze, commonly used of armaments at the time, hints of the judgment and wrath of God.

(7) His voice

> His voice was "like the voice of a multi-
> tude" (v. 6). Revelation 1:15 describes it as
> "the sound of many waters."

> Daniel saw the Almighty revealed in a vision
> representing His holiness, sovereignty, glory, om-
> nipotence, omniscience, and judgment.

2. His extensive authority

> Since Christ is the Commander in Chief of the angel-
> ic army and has all authority (Matt. 28:18), it was
> fitting that He appear to Daniel at this time. Daniel
> was about to receive a prophecy concerning angelic
> warfare that would stretch from his own time to the
> battle described in Revelation 12, in which Michael
> and the holy angels defeat the demonic forces.

This vision must have been a source of great hope for the
aged prophet. His heart had been heavy, but God Himself
appeared to him.

III. THE REACTION TO THE VISION (vv. 7-9)

A. Of Those with Daniel (v. 7)

> "I, Daniel, alone saw the vision; for the men that were
> with me saw not the vision, but a great quaking fell
> upon them, so that they fled to hide themselves."

When heaven invades earth it always leaves man in
awe. Though those with Daniel saw no vision they
knew something was happening and began to shake.
They fled to hide from the presence of God because it
was more than they could bear—a natural response of
sinful man, as seen many times in Scripture.

1. Compared to Job

   When a good man like Job saw God he was forced
   to declare, "I have heard of thee by the hearing of
   the ear, but now mine eye seeth thee. Wherefore I
   abhor myself, and repent in dust and ashes" (Job
   42:5-6).

2. Compared to Isaiah

   Isaiah was a godly man, yet when he saw God he
   said, "Woe is me! For I am undone, because I am a
   man of unclean lips, and I dwell in the midst of a
   people of unclean lips; for mine eyes have seen the
   King, the Lord of hosts" (Isa. 6:5).

3. Compared to Peter

   When Peter saw the power of Jesus displayed he responded, "Depart from me; for I am a sinful man, O
   Lord" (Luke 5:8).

4. Compared to mankind in the Tribulation

   When men realize the great day of God's wrath
   during the Tribulation, they will cry out "to the
   mountains and rocks, Fall on us, and hide us from
   the face of him that sitteth on the throne, and from
   the wrath of the Lamb" (Rev. 6:16). The unholy are
   devastated in the presence of absolute holiness.

B. Of Daniel Himself (vv. 8-9)

   "I was left alone, and saw this great vision, and there
   remained no strength in me; for my comeliness was turned
   in me into corruption, and I retained no strength. Yet
   heard I the voice of his words; and when I heard the voice
   of his words, then was I in a deep sleep on my face, and
   my face toward the ground."

   Daniel was left alone and experienced severe distress—he
   too wasn't able to handle much of God's presence. That his
   "comeliness was turned . . . into corruption" (v. 8) means

he lost his strength and acquired the death-like pallor of one in absolute panic.

On top of that he "heard the voice of [God's] words" (v. 9). That caused him to faint. He was shattered by the voice of God's Son—completely mastered by the awe of His presence. Christ then departed, and Daniel saw Him no more.

IV.  THE MESSENGER FROM HEAVEN (vv. 10-13)

"Behold, an hand touched me, which set me upon my knees and upon the palms of my hands. And he said unto me, O Daniel, a man greatly beloved, understand the words I speak to thee, and stand upright; for unto thee am I now sent. And when he had spoken this word unto me, I stood trembling. He said unto me, Fear not, Daniel; for from the first day that thou didst set thine heart to understand, and to chasten thyself before thy God, thy words were heard, and I am come for thy words. But the prince of the kingdom of Persia withstood me one and twenty days; but, lo, Michael, one of the chief princes, came to help me; and I remained there with the kings of Persia."

A. He Revived Daniel

Almost immediately an angel in the form of a man helped Daniel, who was eighty-five years old and weakened by fasting. The angel enabled him to rise shakily to his hands and knees.

---

**Are You Awed in the Presence of God?**

Daniel's reaction to the presence of God ought to cause us to examine our own attitude towards His presence. Are we awed in His presence? I find myself rushing in and out of God's presence with no thought for His majesty. When I come to worship, too often it seems that my thoughts are focused on the world or some project completely unrelated to God, when I ought to be drained of strength because of overwhelming thoughts of Him. How about you?

## B. He Reassured Daniel

God doesn't make personal appearances to everyone. But Daniel was "greatly beloved." He was a special man, like others named in the Bible: David was called "a man after [God's] own heart" (1 Sam. 13:14), Abraham was called God's friend (Isa. 41:8), the apostle John was "the disciple whom Jesus loved" (John 21:7), and Mary was "highly favored" by God (Luke 1:28). Those who especially delight in God and obey Him become greatly beloved by Him. The angel may have told Daniel he was beloved by God to relieve his fear—he wasn't going to be judged but blessed.

## C. He Was Temporarily Hindered from Seeing Daniel

Daniel had set his heart on understanding why his people had not returned to the land, so he fasted and prayed for a lengthy period of time (vv. 2-3). God's messenger first reassured Daniel not to fear. He wasn't to think God didn't care about his prayers because of the twenty-one days it took to send an answer. In reality, from the first day Daniel mourned he was heard, but delivery of God's answer was delayed.

The angel explained that he—a holy angel from God's presence—had been detained by the "prince of the kingdom of Persia" (v. 13). The ruling kingdom at that time was Persia, but the prince spoken of here was not a man: he was a demon. His position was to influence the events in Persia so that God's plans for the future of Israel would be hindered. Therefore he must have been evil. He must have been an angelic being to be able to fight the archangel Michael (v. 13), and his relationship with Persia was of an ongoing nature since the angel speaking to Daniel would be fighting him again (v. 20).

### The Demons and World Power

Satan has a sophisticated world organization: an unseen network of demons influencing the events of human history. Just as there was a demon assigned to Persia (v. 13), there was another assigned to Greece (v. 20). Psalm 96:5 says, "All the gods of the nations are idols," and demons are behind the false gods people worship (1 Cor. 10:20). Throughout world history demons have been active behind the scenes in an attempt to thwart God's plans.

God sent Michael—a super-angel—to release His messenger from conflict. Michael is mentioned three times in Daniel (Dan. 10:13, 21; 12:1) and two times in the New Testament (Jude 9; Rev. 12:7). He is called "the archangel" (Jude 9), which means "first angel." The name Michael means "one who is of God." In Revelation 12:7 he appears with a host of angels during the Great Tribulation to destroy all demonic forces and win the final battle.

After his struggle with the prince of Persia, Daniel's angelic messenger remained "with the kings of Persia" (Dan. 10:13). He remained as an influence for God with the kings of Persia. That indicates God has assigned holy angels to nations to carry out His purposes. In this continual warfare I often wonder what's happening behind the scenes in our own nation.

VI.   THE PURPOSE OF THE VISION (vv. 14-21)

A. To Prepare Daniel to Receive Extensive Revelation (vv. 14-20a)

"I am come to make thee understand what shall befall thy people in the latter days; for yet the vision is for many days. And when he had spoken such words unto me, I set my face toward the ground, and I became dumb. And, behold, one like the similitude of the sons of men touched my lips; then I opened my mouth, and spoke, and said unto him who stood before me, O my Lord, by the vision my sorrows are turned upon me, and I have retained no strength. For how can the servant of this my lord talk with this my lord? For as for me, straightway there remained no strength in me, neither is there breath left in me. Then there came again and touched me one like the appearance of a man, and he strengthened me, and said, O man greatly beloved, fear not. Peace be unto thee; be strong, yea, be strong. And when he had spoken unto me, I was strengthened, and said, Let my lord speak; for thou hast strengthened me. Then said he, Knowest thou why I come unto thee?"

According to Daniel 10:14 the angel came to give Daniel a vision that would cover a lengthy time span. Specifically, it goes from the time of Daniel to the reign of the Antichrist in the Tribulation. That caused Daniel to lose his strength and voice and fall to the ground for a second time (Dan. 10:15). Such was the effect of so grand a revelation.

In response to Daniel's physical collapse another angel appeared and touched Daniel's lips, which enabled him to speak (v. 16). Daniel told his angelic messenger that he didn't think he would be able to receive a revelation in his weakened condition (v. 17), so another angel came and miraculously strengthened him (v. 18). Daniel then willingly received the revelation (v. 19).

Daniel needed to be strengthened—he had stood before the living God. He may have been the most godly man living at that time, but was devastated when personally confronted by God. We can expect even worse when we face God unless we are protected by the blood of Jesus Christ through faith in Him.

Once Daniel had been strengthened, the angelic messenger asked, "Knowest thou why I come unto thee?" (v. 20)—a question that implies Daniel didn't realize the extent of revelation he was to receive. Daniel had spent twenty-one days asking about the immediate future of his people, but was going to receive a revelation of their future to the end of the age!

## Plumb the Depths!

Daniel prayed for an answer to an immediate dilemma but was given an answer that went far beyond his current focus. He was shown that demons and holy angels carry on warfare, and he experienced the majestic presence of the uncreated Christ—the commander of the angelic hosts. Daniel's summation that the revelation was one of great conflict was accurate (Dan. 10:1, NASB).

Sometimes Christians forget the great works and eternal truths of God and focus on petty things. While God wants us to focus on His kingdom, we too often focus on the mundane (cf. Matt. 6:33). Some Christians never seriously study their Bibles. They become caught up in churchianity—which isn't Christianity at all. We need to be committed to plumbing the depths of God's Word. Then, like Daniel, we'll receive more than we ask for.

### B. To Reassure Daniel of the Truth of Revelation (vv. 20b-21)

"Now will I return to fight with the prince of Persia; and when I am gone forth, lo, the prince of Greece shall come. But I will show thee that which is noted in the scripture of truth; and there is none that holdeth with me in these things, but Michael your prince."

After delivering his message to Daniel, the angel was to return to fighting the prince of Persia on Israel's behalf. God uses angelic conflict to accomplish His will. And once that conflict ended the angel would begin fighting the prince of Greece—the next great world power. Yet the angel reassured Daniel that the message he was about to give was true and that though only Michael was with him, they were sufficient to handle any opposition. What a comfort! Michael must be a magnificent being, for he's the prince of God's people.

### Conclusion

Daniel 10 is a rich portion of Scripture. It gives us insight into God's holiness, majesty, and glory; the preincarnate Christ; and the reality of angelic warfare. Before us are laid open the heart and life of a man without equal: Daniel, the man of prayer. We see that the core of intercessory prayer is a broken and selfless heart, and that the first response to any crisis ought to be prayer. We also see the condescension of God in willingly revealing His truth to man. We see the grace of God in taking a weak and frail man and with a touch making him speak as a prophet. That ought to give us all great comfort. God can use any of us. He is able to take our greatest weaknesses and lift us from uselessness to strength. What a glorious blessing!

## Focusing on the Facts

1. What time period do Daniel 8 and Daniel 10-12 deal with (see p. 60)?
2. How was Daniel's prayer of chapter 9 answered in the same year he prayed (see p. 60)?
3. What discouraged Daniel (see p. 61)?
4. Why might Daniel not have returned to Judea (see p. 61)?
5. Why is it best to translate Daniel 10:1 as referring to a time of great conflict or warfare (see p. 62)?
6. Through what special season of celebration did Daniel mourn and fast (see p. 62).
7. Where did a vision similar to the one recorded in Daniel 10:5-6 occur? Whom were they of (see p. 64)?
8. Describe the appearance of the person in Daniel's vision. What do Daniel's representations of that person's appearance seem to symbolize (see pp. 64-66)?
9. Why was it fitting that the Commander in Chief of the angelic army appear to Daniel when He did (see p. 66)?
10. What reaction did the men with Daniel have when the vision began? What was Daniel's reaction (see pp. 66-68)?
11. In what form did the angel appear who revived Daniel (see p. 68)?
12. What reassurance did the angel give Daniel (see p. 69)?
13. Who detained the holy angel that appeared to Daniel, and why did he do so (see p. 69)?
14. Who came and released God's messenger from conflict (see p. 70)?
15. According to Daniel 10:14 why did the angel come to Daniel (see p. 71)?
16. What are some important insights contained in Daniel 10 (see p. 72)?

## Pondering the Principles

1. Do you automatically face difficulties by persistent prayer as Daniel did, or do you immediately seek human solutions based on human wisdom? Beyond praying for answers in your own trials, do you respond with prayer for others when they are in difficulty? Daniel's prayers were typified

by a selfless concern for others. Take time now to pray for those you know who are in difficulty and need God's answer for what they face.

2. It's easy to become distracted by details and lose one's sense of purpose and direction. The same is true in our understanding of Scripture: when we become interested in only small portions or issues in Scripture, we won't see the panorama of God's purposes displayed by a view of the whole. Make it a point to read through the Bible at least once a year to maintain your view of the Bible's "big picture." To assist you, find someone you can be accountable to on a daily basis to accomplish that goal.

# 5

# The Reign of Rebellion—Part 1

### Outline

Introduction

A. The Chastening of Israel
B. The Protection of Israel

Lesson
I.   Ahasuerus (v. 2)
II.  Alexander the Great (vv. 3-8)
     A. The Extent of His Dominion
     B. The Division of His Empire
     C. The Resulting Conflict
III. Antiochus the Great (vv. 9-20)
     A. Revenge from the North (vv. 9-10)
     B. Retaliation from the South (vv. 11-12)
     C. The Return of the North (vv. 13-20)
        1. The Attack (vv. 13-15)
        2. The Aftermath (vv. 16-20)
IV.  Antiochus Epiphanes (vv. 21-35)
     A. His Accession (vv. 21-24)
     B. His Aggression (vv. 25-35)
        1. The first attack (vv. 25-28)
        2. The second attack (vv. 29-35)
           a) Against Egypt (vv. 29-30)
           b) Against Israel (vv. 31-35)
              (1) Israel's desolation
              (2) Israel's defense

Conclusion

# Introduction

We live in a rebellious age. Daniel 11 chronicles an age of defiance towards God—a defiance that will last through our own time to the return of the Lord Jesus Christ.

### A. The Chastening of Israel

Within the larger context of the world's rebellion against God we read of Israel's rebellion against Him. The Old Testament affirms that Israel is God's chosen nation. Yet it also chronicles its disobedience to Him through idolatry and immorality. It defied God, spurning His grace and lovingkindness. As a result God has chastened Israel.

The chastening of Israel sets the context for Daniel 11. The prophet Jeremiah declared Israel would be punished by spending seventy years in captivity. While in captivity the prophet Daniel realized the seventy years were nearly over and expected the Jewish people to return to their land, Jerusalem to be restored, and the Temple rebuilt. But when permitted to return, only a small fragment of the people made the trip to the Promised Land. Jerusalem remained in disrepair and the Temple in ruins. Instead of responding to God's chastening, they remained entrenched in the pagan lifestyle of Babylon. The seventy-year exile in Babylon was obviously only the beginning of Israel's chastening.

Daniel was discouraged by what he saw and turned to God in prayer. He wanted to know why things hadn't turned out the way he expected. After mourning with fasting and prayer for three weeks, Daniel received the prophecy contained in Daniel 11-12. He was told that the chastening of Israel would continue until the nation was completely restored. At that time the Messiah will establish His kingdom on earth.

## B. The Protection of Israel

Daniel 11:1 says, "I [the messenger angel], in the first year of Darius, the Mede, even I, stood to confirm and to strengthen [the archangel Michael]." Michael had helped out that angel about three years previously (Dan. 10:1) when the decree allowing the Jewish people to return to their land was issued. Apparently the demon named "the prince of Persia" (Dan. 10:13) was trying to prevent that return, and that's why Michael needed assistance. That gives us insight into how the holy angels enforce God's will in the midst of demonic activity.

The messenger angel brought a revelation of God's future plans for His people. Though Daniel was told that his people would continue to suffer through the tribulation until the establishment of the millennial kingdom (Dan. 12:2), it was a comfort for him to know that his people would be under the protection of God's holy angels throughout that period.

### Daniel in the Critics' Den

Though the prophecy in Daniel 11 deals with the rise and fall of Gentile world powers, it's primarily concerned with the suffering and fate of Israel. The minute details of the prophecy have already been fulfilled in history with an accuracy that has attracted the attacks of literary critics. It so precisely predicted future events involving the Persian and Greek Empires that critics assume Daniel must have been written after the events took place. That's based on the premise that God didn't write the Bible and they must thus conclude that the author of the book of Daniel was a liar, since he claimed to receive knowledge of future events from God prior to their actually happening. They are left with a God who doesn't know the future and a prophet of impeccable character (Ezek. 14:14, 20) who in fact behaved dishonorably. But there are many linguistic and historical reasons that authenticate the book of Daniel as prophecy. (For further information see Josh McDowell's *Daniel in the Critics' Den*, available from Josh McDowell Ministries, P.O. Box 1000, Dallas, TX 75221; 1-800-222-JOSH). Daniel wasn't a liar, and our God is able to tell us about the future as easily as if it were the past.

# Lesson

## I. AHASUERUS (v. 2)

"There shall stand up yet three kings in Persia; and the fourth shall be far richer than they all, and by his strength through his riches he shall stir up all against the realm of Greece."

The angel told Daniel that three Persian kings would precede a fourth, who would be stronger and richer than the others. He would attack Greece. Historically that's exactly what happened: though there were more than four Persian kings in the history of Persia, from the time of Daniel there were four, the last of whom mounted a massive assault on Greece.

The first was named Cambyses, the son of Cyrus, who was king at the time Daniel's prophecy was given (ca. 537 B.C.; cf. Dan. 10:1). The second was a man named pseudo-Smerdis who looked so much like Cambyses that he was able to usurp the throne by deception. The third king was Darius Hystaspes, who launched a minor unsuccessful attack on Greece. The fourth was King Ahasuerus, also known as Xerxes I. He is the Persian king spoken of in the book of Esther. He had fabulous wealth and commanded one of the largest military forces ever assembled in the ancient world. With his huge army and navy he attacked Greece but was soundly defeated by the Greeks on both land and sea. The Greeks never forgot that attack, and 150 years later took revenge on the Persians through Alexander the Great.

## II. ALEXANDER THE GREAT (vv. 3-8)

"A mighty king shall stand up, that shall rule with great dominion, and do according to his will. And when he shall stand up, his kingdom shall be broken, and shall be divided toward the four winds of heaven, and not to his posterity, nor according to his dominion which he ruled; for his kingdom shall be plucked up, even for others beside those. And the king of the south shall be strong, and one of his princes; and he shall be strong above him, and have dominion; his dominion shall be a great dominion. And in the end of years they shall join themselves together; for the king's daughter of the south shall come to the king of the north to make an agreement. But she shall not retain the power of the arm, neither shall he stand, nor his arm; but she shall be given up, and they that brought her, and he that begot her, and he that strengthened her in these times. But out of a branch of her roots shall one stand up in his estate, who shall come with an army, and shall enter into the fortress of the king of the north, and shall deal against them, and shall prevail; and shall also carry captives into Egypt their gods, with their princes, and with their precious vessels of silver and of gold; and he shall continue more years than the king of the north."

## A. The Extent of His Dominion

— The "mighty king" of verse 3 was Alexander the Great of Greece. That is affirmed by the vast majority of Bible commentators. He retaliated for the previous Persian incursions into Greece by seizing the entire Persian Empire. He conquered the western world from Greece to India, and then wept that there were no other kingdoms for him to conquer. He was a man of "great dominion" (v. 3) and may have had a more significant impact on history than any other ruler. He was an absolute monarch with a powerful personality, great leadership ability, and a powerful army. With those assets he was able to "do according to his will" (v. 3). Israel was part of the Persian Empire at the time of Alexander's conquest, so in occupying the empire Alexander took possession of Israel.

## B. The Division of His Empire

Alexander died at the age of thirty-three. No sooner did he "stand up" (v. 4) in the power of his empire than he was struck down. His empire shattered and "divided toward the four winds of heaven" (v. 4)—among his four generals. As Daniel 11 predicted, the empire did not go to "his posterity" (v. 4) nor remain "according to his dominion which he ruled" (v. 4).

Alexander's heirs were a mentally retarded half-brother, an illegitimate child, and a baby born after Alexander's death. They were all murdered. After a struggle for power General Cassander took Macedonia and Greece, General Lysimachus took Thrace and Asia Minor, General Seleucus took Syria (to the north of Israel), and General Ptolomy took Egypt (to the south of Israel). The dominion of each was less than that of Alexander—just as Daniel prophesied.

## C. The Resulting Conflict

Seleucus and Ptolomy produced the dynasties that Daniel 11:5-20 focuses on. The two dynasties were often at war, and since Israel was located between them, their wars were often fought in Israel or on its borders. In those verses are recorded two centuries of conflict in which Israel was a pawn between the Ptolemaic kings in the south and the Seleucid kings to the north.

Initially, the Ptolemaic dynasty was more powerful than the Seleucid, but as time went on the northern dynasty increased in power. The two kingdoms determined to resolve increasing tension between them by an alliance. Berenice, the daughter of Ptolemy II Philadelphus (the king of the south), married Antiochus II Theos (the grandson of Seleucus, the king of the north). That was a common method of cementing together alliances in the ancient world. Unfortunately, Antiochus was already married, but he divorced his wife and went ahead with marriage to Berenice in about 250 B.C. That's exactly what the angel told Daniel would happen (Dan. 11:5-6).

The marriage did not produce any lasting peace: after the death of Ptolemy II Philadelphus, Antiochus II Theos divorced Berenice and took back his former wife, Laodice. Laodice took revenge by murdering Berenice, her son, and her attendants. She also murdered Antiochus (thus completely fulfilling verse 6). Those murders brought Laodice's son, Seleucus II Callinicus, to the throne in 246 B.C.

Berenice did not remain unavenged. The angel told Daniel, "Out . . . of her roots shall one stand up in his estate, who shall come with an army, and shall enter into the fortress of the king of the north, and shall deal against them and prevail" (v. 7). Berenice's brother Ptolemy III Euergetes, the king of Egypt at the time of Berenice's murder, brought an army against Callinicus and defeated him. As a result the angel's statement that he would "carry captive into Egypt their gods, with their princes, and with their precious vessels of silver and gold" (v. 8) came true. History records that Ptolemy returned to Egypt with hundreds of idol statues and thousands of talents in silver.

Callinicus died from a riding accident about 226 B.C. Ptolemy III reigned in Egypt for six years after that, for the angel told Daniel that he would "continue more years than the king of the north" (v. 8). The precise way in which these prophecies were fulfilled points to the accuracy of Scripture. It also points to the continued suffering of Israel as it sat in the middle of those two warring dynasties.

III.  ANTIOCHUS THE GREAT (vv. 9-20)

Liberal and conservative scholars agree that the next great king was Antiochus III the Great.

A. Revenge from the North (vv. 9-10)

"The king of the south shall come into his kingdom, and shall return into his own land. But his sons shall be stirred up, and shall assemble a multitude of great forces; and one shall certainly come, and overflow, and pass through; then shall he return, and be stirred up, even to his fortress."

Ptolemy had defeated Callinicus, the northern king, so he now controlled Israel. But Callinicus had two sons (v. 10). They raised "a multitude of great forces" (v. 10) to avenge their father's defeat—but one (Seleucus III Soter) died. The remaining son (Antiochus III the Great) became king of the north and continued the campaign against the south. He swept through Israel with a force of about 75,000 soldiers and penetrated all the way to a southern fortress.

B. Retaliation from the South (vv. 11-12)

"The king of the south shall be moved with anger, and shall come forth and fight with him, even with the king of the north; and he shall set forth a great multitude, but the multitude shall be given into his hand. And when he hath taken away the multitude, his heart shall be lifted up; and he shall cast down many ten thousands, but he shall not be strengthened by it."

At the time of Antiochus's invasion Ptolemy IV Philopator was the king of the south. In response to the invasion Ptolemy raised an army of 70,000 infantry, 5,000 calvary, and 73 elephants (which were used as beasts of burden and battering rams). Ptolemy was successful, and the multitude from the north was "given into his hand" (v. 11). History records that Antiochus lost 10,000 infantry, 300 cavalry, and five elephants. But Ptolemy was not strengthened by his victory—in the long run he only made Antiochus angry.

C. The Return of the North (vv. 13-20)

1. The Attack (vv. 13-15)

"The king of the north shall return, and shall set forth a multitude greater than the former, and shall certainly come, after certain years, with a great army and with much riches. And in those times there shall many stand up against the king of the south; also the robbers of thy people shall exalt themselves to establish the vision, but they shall fall. So the king of the north shall come, and cast up a siege mound, and take the fortified cities; and the arms of the south shall not withstand, neither his chosen people, neither shall there be any strength to withstand."

Thirteen years after his defeat by Ptolemy, Antiochus returned to fight Egypt with "a multitude greater than the former" (v. 13). His army was assisted by "the robbers of [Daniel's] people" (v. 14). The Hebrew word translated "robbers" literally means "sons of breaking." It refers to violent men among the Jewish people who broke the covenant law of God—apostates. They were revolutionaries who joined the cause of Antiochus as mercenaries. They apparently thought that by aiding Antiochus he would give the Jewish people their freedom. But the angel told Daniel respecting their goal, "They shall fall" (v. 14).

In 199 B.C. Antiochus's forces routed the southern army in Palestine (v. 15).

2. The Aftermath (vv. 16-20)

"He that cometh against him shall do according to his own will, and none shall stand before him; and he shall stand in the glorious land, which by his hand shall be consumed. He shall also set his face to enter with the strength of his whole kingdom, and upright ones with him; thus shall he do; and he shall give him the daughter of women, corrupting her, but she shall not stand on his side, neither be for him. After this shall he turn his face unto the coasts, and shall take many, but a prince on his own behalf shall cause the reproach offered by him to cease; without his own reproach, he shall cause it to turn upon him. Then he shall turn his face toward the fortress of his own land, but he shall stumble and fall, and not be found. Then shall stand up in his estate a raiser of taxes in the glory of the kingdom, but within a few days he shall be destroyed, neither in anger, nor in battle."

Antiochus the Great's entry into "the glorious land"— the land of Israel—did not result in freedom for Israel. Antiochus treated the Jewish mercenaries who joined him with favor and paid them well. But he took longlasting control over Palestine, contrary to their wishes.

Antiochus decided to consolidate and strengthen his power by an alliance with Egypt. He offered "the daughter of women" (a phrase probably used to express high feminine charm) to the Egyptian king in marriage as a gesture of good faith. That woman was his daughter, the lovely Cleopatra (not the one associated with Julius Caesar and Marc Antony). Antiochus intended that she act as a spy ("corrupting her"—v. 17) at the Egyptian court, but the angel told Daniel, "She shall not stand on [Antiochus's] side, neither be for him" (v. 17). Cleopatra loved her husband more than her father.

## History Is His Story

The prophecy in Daniel 11 is replete with seemingly inconsequential details. Perhaps you wonder why they're in the Bible. One reason is to show us God's control of history. He determines the boundaries of nations. He knows history from the beginning to the end because history is, quite literally, "His story."

Once Antiochus achieved control of Palestine, his desire for conquest shifted toward "the coasts" (v. 18)—the Mediterranean islands and Greece. But that was an area in which Rome had an interest, and Antiochus was defeated in battle by a Roman army in 191 B.C. As a result Antiochus was forced to return to "the fortress of his own land" (v. 19). There he was murdered when he tried to plunder a temple dedicated to Jupiter.

Antiochus the Great was succeeded by his son Seleucus IV Philopater, who became a "raiser of taxes" (v. 20). That's because he was forced to pay Rome one thousand talents annually in reparation for injuries caused by his father's battles. His short reign was ended when he was "destroyed, neither in anger, nor in battle" (v. 20): he was assassinated by his prime minister in 176 B.C. The details of Daniel's prophecy were fulfilled precisely!

## IV. ANTIOCHUS EPIPHANES (vv. 21-35)

### A. His Accession (vv. 21-24)

"In his estate shall stand up a vile person, to whom they shall not give the honor of the kingdom; but he shall come in peaceably, and obtain the kingdom by flatteries. And with the arms of a flood shall they be overflown from before him, and shall be broken; yea, also the prince of the covenant. And after the league made with him he shall work deceitfully; for he shall come up, and shall become strong with a small people. He shall enter peaceably even upon the fattest places of the province, and he shall do that which his fathers have not done, nor his fathers' fathers; he shall scatter among them the prey, and spoil, and riches; yea, and he shall plot against the strongholds, even for a time."

Antiochus Epiphanes, the next northern king, was "a vile person" (v. 21). He obtained the throne by deceit and flattery in 175 B.C. He was the younger son of Antiochus the Great and had no claim to the throne. His nephew ought to have been installed as king but was held hostage in Rome.

Antiochus devastated the Egyptians and their boy king Ptolemy VI Philometor. (The battle is described more fully in verses 25-27.) He accomplished that by initially adopting a policy of friendship with Egypt while at the same time deceitfully plotting against it (v. 23). In his own territories he entered "upon the fattest places" (v. 24), despoiling the rich and then distributing gifts to the poor—he was a self-styled Robin Hood. That gained him popular support. He also did everything possible to undermine strong communities in his kingdom so there would be no challenge to his power. He quickly put down any move against him.

## B. His Aggression (vv. 25-35)

### 1. The first attack (vv. 25-28)

"He shall stir up his power and his courage against the king of the south with a great army; and the king of the south shall be stirred up to battle with a very great and mighty army, but he shall not stand; for they shall plot against him. Yea, they that feed of the portion of his food shall destroy him, and his army shall overthrow, and many shall fall down slain. And both these kings' hearts shall be to do mischief, and they shall speak lies at one table, but it shall not prosper; for yet the end shall be at the time appointed. Then shall he return into his land with great riches, and his heart shall be against the holy covenant; and he shall do exploits, and return to his own land."

In 170 B.C. Antiochus's army was victorious over Ptolemy's larger Egyptian army at the battle of Pelusium. Antiochus was victorious in part because Ptolemy's counselors plotted against him (vv. 25-26). The angel told Daniel that because of the betrayal, "his army shall overflow, and many shall fall down slain" (v. 26).

Following Egypt's defeat the two kings sat down together and spoke "lies at one table" (v. 27). Their promises to each other were not intended to be fulfilled—like so many of the world's worthless treaties. The goals of the two kings remained unfulfilled because they didn't coincide with the "end" God had in mind. That end would come in God's "appointed time" in the future.

Antiochus failed to obtain complete control of Egypt because Rome intervened. Instead he turned his army north and marched through Israel. Daniel was told that Antiochus's heart "shall be against the holy covenant; and he shall do exploits" (v. 28). He pillaged the land and sacked Jerusalem, killing many

Jewish people and causing terrible suffering. He then continued north "to his own land" (v. 28).

2. **The second attack (vv. 29-35)**

   *a)* **Against Egypt (vv. 29-30)**

   "At the time appointed, he shall return, and come toward the south; but it shall not be as the former, or as the latter. For the ships of Kittim shall come against him; therefore, he shall be grieved, and return, and have indignation against the holy covenant; so shall he do; he shall even return, and have intelligence with those who forsake the holy covenant."

   Many of us are familiar with movies in which, during a fight between the cowboys and Indians, a distant trumpet is heard and then the cavalry comes charging over the hill. Verse 30 gives us a similar scenario: Antiochus returned with another army to attack Egypt, but the Ptolemies had enlisted the aid of Rome. "The ships of Kittim" refers to the arrival of a Roman fleet that effectively deterred Antiochus in his attack on Egypt.

   Angry and disappointed, Antiochus turned his army north. In route he vented his anger against those of "the holy covenant" (v. 30)—the faithful Jewish people. There he was supported by those Jews who had forsaken the holy covenant.

   *b)* **Against Israel (vv. 31-35)**

   "Forces shall stand on his part, and they shall pollute the sanctuary of strength, and shall take away the daily sacrifice, and they shall place the abomination that maketh desolate. And such as do wickedly against the covenant shall he corrupt by flatteries; but the people that do know their God shall be strong, and do exploits. And they that understand among the people shall instruct many; yet they shall fall by the sword, and by flame, by captivity, and by spoil, many days. Now when they shall fall, they shall be helped with a little help; but many shall cling to them with flatteries. And some of them of understanding shall fall, to test them, and to purge, and to make them white, even to the time of the end, because it is yet for a time appointed."

(1) Israel's desolation

In Jerusalem Antiochus placed guards around the Temple to prevent worship. On a particular Sabbath he ordered that women and children be slaughtered. He required idolatrous worship and held Greek athletic contests (in which the athletes competed while naked) in full view of the Temple. Greek culture was imposed, a statue of the Greek god Zeus erected in the Temple, a pig (a ceremonially unclean animal) sacrificed on the Temple altar, and the priests were forced to eat pork from the sacrifice. All those abominations were intended to desecrate the Jewish Temple.

Although Antiochus's actions were supported by apostate Jews, Daniel was told that "the people that do know their God shall be strong, and do exploits" (v. 32). Those who resisted Antiochus were subjected to his persecutions—typical of the persecutions by the Antichrist described in the New Testament. Their suffering was "by the sword, and by flame, by captivity, and by spoil" (v. 33).

(2) Israel's defense

In response to those persecutions arose a group of Jewish people called the Hasidim. They were upholders of the law according to the apocryphal book of 1 Maccabees (2:42). Their leader was Judas Maccabeus, who led a revolt from 168-165 B.C. His revolt "helped with a little help" (v. 34)—but was only a temporary respite from Syrian persecution. He did take bloody revenge against those Jews who had helped Antiochus, but like many revolutions, many who identified with the Maccabean revolt joined only for personal gain.

God allowed His people to be persecuted "to test them, and to purge, and to make them white" (v. 35). He wanted His people purified from sin as metal is refined from impurities. Nothing drives people to God like suffering. A person's thoughts tend to go straight up when he is faced with imminent destruction.

Daniel received an astonishingly complete revelation from God concerning the future suffering of the Jewish people "even to the time of the end." They would suffer through the Persian, Greek, and Roman Empires. And they would continue to suffer up through the time of the revived Roman Empire and its ruler, the Antichrist.

## God's Persistent Love for Israel

God has ordained all of history from first to last. He has determined history's notable events and its minutest happenings. He is not finished with refining Israel, and that explains why the Jewish people continue to suffer.

God is faithful to Israel in spite of her refusal to turn to Him. Our Lord said of Israel, "Ye will not come to me, that ye might have life" (John 5:40). Jesus wept over Jerusalem, saying, "Jerusalem, Jerusalem, thou that killest the prophets, and stonest them who are sent unto thee, how often would I have gathered thy children together, even as a hen gathereth her chickens under her wings, and ye would not!" (Matt. 23:37). Paul echoed God's words through Isaiah, "All day long have I stretched forth my hands unto a disobedient and contrary people" (Rom. 10:21).

Israel's suffering is according to God's grace. Though He has every right to forget them—to write them off for their constant spiritual harlotries, disobedience, abuse of privileges, and covenant breaking—He doesn't. God will continue the purging process until "the time of the end . . . a time appointed" (Dan. 11:35).

There will come a time when "all Israel shall be saved" (Rom. 11:26). That's a great promise! All during the time of Israel's chastening the archangel Michael has watched over them, and the time will come when he will fight for them (Dan. 12:1). The Spirit of God will descend upon Israel, they'll be redeemed, and will receive their kingdom (Zech. 12:10).

## Conclusion

I hope you have a heart for the Jewish people. Among them are an elect remnant who believe in the Lord Jesus Christ, and God calls every believer to reach out to them. An old missionary hymn puts it this way:

> Shall we whose souls are lighted with wisdom from on high;
> Shall we to souls benighted the lamp of life deny?

## Focusing on the Facts

1. How long will man's defiance of God last (see p. 76)?
2. How does the Old Testament say Israel disobeyed God? What has that resulted in (see p. 76)?
3. Explain the context of Daniel 11 (see p. 76).
4. Describe what kind of answer Daniel received to his prayers as given in Daniel 11-12 (see p. 76).
5. In the midst of demonic activity, what are God's holy angels doing (see p. 77)?
6. Describe the attacks of literary critics on the book of Daniel. What is their basic presupposition (see p. 77)?
7. Who was the fourth Persian king who led a major attack on Greece? In what other book of the Bible does he appear, and under what name (see p. 78)?
8. When the Greeks finally retaliated against the Persians for the attacks made on them, who led them? Describe his success (see p. 79).

9. What happened to the Greek Empire after its great leader died (see pp. 79-80)?

10. Identify the two dynasties identified as "the king of the south" and "the king of the north" in chapter 11 (see p. 80).

11. How did the two kingdoms attempt to resolve increasing tension between them (see p. 80)?

12. What two realities does the minute fulfillment of prophecy in Daniel point to (see p. 81)?

13. After his initial unsuccessful campaign against Egypt, what did Antiochus the Great do thirteen years later? Who assisted him (see pp. 82-83)?

14. How did Antiochus attempt to establish a deceptive alliance with Egypt? Why did it fail (see p. 84)?

15. Who was the "vile" successor to Antiochus the Great? How did he obtain the throne (Dan. 11:21; see p. 85)?

16. After failing to obtain control of Egypt in 170 B.C., what did Antiochus Epiphanes do (see pp. 86-87)?

17. What deterred Antiochus Epiphanes in his second attack on Egypt? How did he vent his anger and disappointment (see p. 87)?

18. What did Antiochus Epiphanes do to the Temple in Jerusalem? What was his persecution of the Jewish people typical of (see p. 88)?

19. What is God's purpose in the persecutions of the Jewish people according to Daniel 11:35 (see p. 89)?

### Pondering the Principles

1. Daniel 11 shows the ongoing chastening of rebellious Israel. Unfortunately, few responded to that discipline. When allowed to return to their land from captivity, many were so entrenched in a pagan lifestyle that they wouldn't leave Babylon. Is that how you respond to the Lord's discipline in your life? A right response to God's gracious dealing with us is reflected in this hymn by Adelaide Pollard:

Have Thine own way, Lord! Have Thine own way!
Thou art the Potter, I am the clay:
Mold me and make me after Thy will,
While I am waiting, yielded and still.

Resolve to adopt the attitude of the hymnwriter in God's
dealings with you.

2. The ultimate purpose of divine testing is to strengthen our
   faith (cf. James 1:2-3). Chastisement may not seem pleasant,
   yet it does affirm God's continuing commitment to us. We
   see that truth in the affirmation that though the Jewish
   people have rebelled against God, "all Israel shall be
   saved" (Rom. 11:26). God has promised us that He will
   never leave or forsake us (Heb. 13:5). Praise God for His
   faithfulness to His own, and ask Him how you may be
   used to bring the light of the gospel to a Jewish person you
   know.

# 6

# The Reign of Rebellion—Part 2

## Outline

Introduction

Review
I.    Ahasuerus (v. 2)
II.   Alexander the Great (vv.3-8)
III.  Antiochus the Great (vv. 9-20)
IV.   Antiochus Epiphanes (vv. 21-35)

Lesson
V.    The Antichrist (vv. 36-45)
   A. The Timing of His Coming
      1.  "The time of the end"
      2.  The scope of the prophecy
      3.  The historical record
      4.  The timing of God's final judgment
      5.  The similarity of description
      6.  The prophetic context
   B. The Circumstances at His Coming
      1.  His character (vv. 36-39)
         a) His power (v. 36a)
         b) His pride (v. 36b)
         c) His blasphemy (v. 36c)
         d) His perversion (v. 37a)
            (1) Of tradition
            (2) Of love
            (3) Of religion
         e) His idol (vv. 37b-39)
            (1) The god he will honor (vv. 37b-38a)
            (2) The offering he will make (vv. 38b-39)

2. His conflict (vv. 40-45)
   a) The cause (v. 40a-b)
      (1) Invasion from the south (v. 40a)
      (2) Invasion from the north (v. 40b)
          (a) Israel will be regathered
          (b) Israel will be at peace
          (c) Israel will be in its latter days
          (d) Israel's enemy will be far north
   b) The chariots (v. 40c)
   c) The conquest (vv. 40d-43)
      (1) Of the Russians (v. 40d)
      (2) Of the Arabs (v. 41)
      (3) Of the Africans (vv. 42-43)
   d) The cataclysm (v. 44)
   e) The climax (v. 45a)
   f) The condemnation (v. 45b)

Conclusion


## Introduction


— Daniel 11 describes God's chastening of His people Israel. Because of their sinfulness Israel was taken captive into Babylon for seventy years. God sent an angel to show Daniel that that chastening will continue through the reign of the Antichrist to the return of the Messiah. Daniel 11:1-35 details the oppression of the land and people of Israel during the Persian and Greek eras.

God desires the spiritual purification of His people (Dan. 11:35). He uses suffering to accomplish that. The apostle Peter told his readers that the Lord would perfect them after they had "suffered awhile" (1 Pet. 5:10). James said that the testing of our faith produces patience, which perfects us (James 1:3-4).


## Review


I.   AHASUERUS (v. 2; see pp. 78)

II.  ALEXANDER THE GREAT(vv.3-8; see pp. 78-81)

III.  ANTIOCHUS THE GREAT (vv. 9-20; see pp. 81-84)

IV.  ANTIOCHUS EPIPHANES (vv. 21-35; see pp. 85-90)

**Lesson**

V.  THE ANTICHRIST (vv. 36-45)

Between verses 35 and 36 of Daniel we leap across centuries of persecutors to the final persecutor of Israel: the Antichrist. He will reign over the final form of the Roman Empire and preside during the final chapter of God's chastisement of Israel.

The Antichrist will be all the evil power of Ahasuerus, Alexander, Antiochus the Great, and Antiochus Epiphanes combined into one person. He will be a counterfeit Christ who will make a treaty with Israel. But in the middle of the seven-year Tribulation period he will break the treaty, desecrate the Temple, forbid the practice of Judaism, blaspheme God, and precipitate the holocaust of Armageddon that will end with the return of Jesus Christ.

A. The Timing of His Coming

The sharp break in the flow of history that occurs at verse 36 is introduced in verse 35: "Even to the time of the end." Up to this point Daniel 11 deals with what to us is past history. Verse 36 onward reveals events that are yet future.

Some Bible commentators disagree. They believe verses 36-45 refer to Antiochus Epiphanes, not the Antichrist. Because they refuse to accept that the Bible predicts future events, they are forced to explain those verses as past history.

There are several reasons to suggest that a king yet future is spoken of in Daniel 11:36-45.

95

1. "The time of the end"

   "The time of the end" (v. 35, cf. v. 40) is an eschatological term that points to the last days of the present age.

2. The scope of the prophecy

   The scope of the prophecy goes beyond the Persian and Greek eras. In Daniel 10:14 the messenger angel tells Daniel, "I am come to make thee understand what shall befall thy people in the latter days."

3. The historical record

   We can substantiate the historical accuracy of the prophecy in Daniel 11 up to verse 35. After that we have no historical data to explain Daniel verses 36-45. Also, there is no indication that the events recorded in those verses were fulfilled during the life of Antiochus Epiphanes.

4. The timing of God's final judgment

   Daniel 11:36 says the king "shall prosper till the indignation be accomplished." When the term "indignation" is used in the Bible in a prophetic context, it is used almost synonymously with the Tribulation period—the final outpouring of God's wrath in the last days.

5. The similarity of description

   The ruler described in this passage is similar to other scriptural accounts of the Antichrist. Daniel 12:1 says he will reign during "a time of trouble, such as never was since there was a nation even to that same time." It will be worse than any other time in the history of man. Verse 2 tells us it will be followed by the resurrection, which is at the end of the last days.

6. The prophetic context

The previous three prophecies in the book of Daniel all speak of the Antichrist. It makes sense that the final prophecy in Daniel would follow the same pattern.

B. The Circumstances at His Coming

1. His character (vv. 36-39)

"The king shall do according to his will; and he shall exalt himself, and magnify himself above every god, and shall speak marvelous things against the God of gods, and shall prosper till the indignation be accomplished; for that which is determined shall be done. Neither shall he regard the gods of his fathers, nor the desire of women, nor regard any god; for he shall magnify himself above all."

This king has been called "the willful king" since he will operate "according to his [own] will." He is identified by several descriptive titles in the Bible: the "little horn" (Dan. 7:8), the "king of fierce countenance" (Dan. 8:23), "the prince that shall come" (Dan. 9:26), the "man of sin . . . the son of perdition" (2 Thess. 2:3—a Hebraism meaning he is doomed to destruction), and "a beast" (Rev. 13:1).

a) His power (v. 36a)

"The king shall do according to his will."

The Antichrist will make his decisions as an absolute sovereign and with self-centered motives. Because he will be empowered by Satan he will give the world the baptism of hell. Because he will have demonic cooperation he will be able to establish an absolute world monarchy. He will have credibility because he will be able to do miraculous signs and wonders that deceive people. Under his rule the Western world will become the protector of Israel against those who

97

desire to control it—the Soviet Union, the East, the Arab nations, and a coalition of African nations.

During the Antichrist's reign there will be other rulers, but he will be supreme over all. Revelation 17 mentions ten other kings who will be puppet kings under the Antichrist. Revelation 13 indicates he will be aided by a "false prophet" who will do his bidding. The kings of the south, north, and east will attempt to revolt against the Antichrist only after his sovereignty is established. But his power to make decisions will be absolute. His influence in the world will be so complete that he will cause all mankind to bear his mark to function in society (Rev. 13:16-17).

*b)* His pride (v. 36*b*)

"He shall exalt himself, and magnify himself above every god."

Antiochus Epiphanes was proud, but he never magnified himself above every god. He religiously worshiped the gods of the Greeks and tried to force the Jews to do the same. But the Antichrist will be atheistic—setting himself above every god. The apostle Paul said he "opposeth and exalteth himself above all that is called God, or that is worshiped, so that he, as God, sitteth in the temple of God, showing himself that he is God" (2 Thess. 2:4). Although there have been many egoists in history, the one who will sit in the Temple claiming to be God will be the greatest of all. He will be the epitome of pride. Paul appropriately identified him as an opposer or adversary (2 Thess. 2:4)—a common description of Satan that directly links the Antichrist to the evil power behind him.

The verb used in 2 Thessalonians 2:4 is translated "exalted above measure" in 2 Corinthians 12:7. The Antichrist will exalt himself above all that is worshiped—whether deities, shrines, images, or altars. He will initially tolerate religion, but at a given time he will destroy the false church (identified as "the great harlot" in Rev. 17:1). He will let the Jewish people worship in their Temple until the middle of the Tribulation but then he will desecrate it—committing the abomination of desolation after the pattern of Antiochus Epiphanes and slaughtering so many Jewish people that two-thirds of them will die (Zech. 13:8).

c) His blasphemy (v. 36c)

"[He] shall speak marvelous things against the God of gods."

The Antichrist will be a blasphemer without equal. Revelation 13:5-6 says, "There was given unto him a mouth speaking great things and blasphemies. . . . And he opened his mouth in blasphemy against God, to blaspheme His name, and His tabernacle, and them that dwell in heaven." His will be the mouth of hell, and he will try to change God's moral laws (Dan. 7:25).

The Hebrew text of Daniel 11:36 indicates that the "marvelous" or astonishing things the Antichrist will speak will be unbelievable. In effect, that means the intensity of his blasphemy will be unparalleled in human history.

## Why Will God Allow the Antichrist to Reign?

God will tolerate the Antichrist's atrocities because they are part of the process God is using to purify Israel. And they will last only a short period of time. Revelation 13:5 states that the Antichrist will be given power for only forty-two months (three-and-a-half years). He will exalt himself as God for the last half of the Tribulation, until God's wrath is completely poured out. His blasphemy and oppression will finally lead the nation of Israel to recognize Jesus Christ as its Messiah and turn to Him. Nothing short of the Antichrist's reign and persecution will do that.

*d*) His perversion (v. 37*a*)

The angel told Daniel that the Antichrist will be perverted in three ways.

(1) Of tradition

"Neither shall he regard the gods of his fathers."

The *KJV* translates that as "the God of his fathers," but it is better translated with the plural "gods" because the singular form of the Hebrew word is used twice in the immediate context. That means the Antichrist will not respect the traditional religion of his forefathers.

Paul said that in the last days men will be "without natural affection" (2 Tim. 3:3). Families will fall apart because people will no longer care about their family members. There will be no respect for parents, heritage, or family tradition. People normally respect the beliefs of their ancestors, the Antichrist will not.

(2) Of love

"Nor the desire of women."

That's a very difficult phrase to interpret. It could mean that the Antichrist will be a homosexual because he will lack the normal capacity to love a woman. Some think it means he will lack the gentleness and graciousness characteristic of women. Others conclude it means he won't care for the Messiah, "the desire of women" being interpreted as the hope of Jewish women to give birth to the Messiah. But in context that last interpretation seems forced since many people don't have that desire and thus it would not sufficiently distinguish the

Antichrist. I believe the phrase indicates that he will not have a normal affection for a wife, mother, or sister.

(3) Of religion

"Nor regard any god."

Most people believe in some kind of god. When getting into trouble they usually turn to a higher source of power than themselves for help. Men invent religions because they naturally believe in the supernatural. But the Antichrist will be completely irreligious.

Our world seems ready for that kind of leader. Many today aren't bothered by a man in leadership who doesn't have normal family relationships, though fifty years ago no one would have considered him. Few now seem to be bothered if a man has a perverted sexual life—homosexuality is often presented merely as an alternative lifestyle. Nor is belief in God thought to be important in our society. Probably most would accept an atheist in power, especially if he pretended to be religious.

e) His idol (vv. 37b-39)

(1) The god he will honor (vv. 37b-38a)

"He shall magnify himself above all. But in his estate [lit. "in its place"] shall he honor the god of fortresses."

The Antichrist will worship "the god of fortresses" in place of having the normal human affections for family, women, and God. The Hebrew word translated "fortresses" is used six other times in Daniel 11 (vv. 1, 7, 10, 19, 31, 39). In each instance it refers to a strong place or fort, and always deals with military power. Daniel 7:23 says the fourth

and final form of the Roman Empire under
the rule of the Antichrist "shall devour the
whole earth, and shall tread it down, and break
it in pieces." Such incredible military power
means he will be able to magnify himself above
all else. He will have the intimidation of nu-
clear weapons or whatever other weapons of
mass destruction are fashionable at his time.

(2)   The offering he will make (vv. 38*b*-39)

"A god whom his fathers knew not shall he
honor with gold, and silver, and with precious stones, and pleasant things. Thus shall
he do in the strongest fortresses with a foreign god, whom he shall acknowledge and
increase with glory; and he shall cause them
to rule over many, and shall divide the land
for gain."

The text assumes that the Antichrist's forefathers would offer anything valuable to their
deities—whether gold, silver, precious
stones, or other desirable items. But the
Antichrist will offer his precious metals and
stones to acquire a war machine, "a god
whom his fathers knew not." Because war is so
expensive he may seek to capture the world's
wealth to buy armaments.

The Antichrist will attack the strongest fortresses with his "foreign god" (war machine). Once he obtains control of the earth
he will honor everyone who honors him
with land, a leadership position, and limited
independence. To insure political control he
will obligate those he conquers to obey him.
That kind of control has been seen in our
time in atheistic Communism—a militant
philosophy of world domination.

2. His conflict (vv. 40-45)

During the first three-and-a-half years of the Tribulation the Antichrist will obtain world dominion. During that time he will let the false church coexist with his atheistic government. He will also allow Israel certain freedoms while he honors his treaty of protection with them. But that will change.

*a*) The cause (v. 40*a-b*)

(1) Invasion from the south (v. 40*a*)

"At the time of the end shall the king of the south push at him."

A revolution against the Antichrist will erupt. Holding a global empire together is an impossible task, and even hell won't be able to do it. The empire the Antichrist obtained peacefully by solving some problems in the Middle East will begin to fall apart. "The king of the south" will bring an army out of Africa in an attempt to control the strategic Middle East. The Hebrew word describing that attack as a "push" comes from a word meaning "to push like a goat."

(2) Invasion from the north (v. 40*b*)

"The king of the north shall come against him like a whirlwind."

At the same time an army more powerful than the southern army will attack from the north. The Antichrist will be in control of the Middle East, so those two attacks will be against him. "The king of the north" refers to the area now occupied by the Soviet Union or Russia, which desires control of the Middle East.

Ezekiel 38-39 contains important evidence indicating that a Russian army will invade from the north:

(a) Israel will be regathered

Ezekiel 38:8 says, "After many days, thou shalt be visited; in the latter years thou shalt come into the land." When the king of the north attacks, Israel will be regathered in its land (cf. v. 12).

(b) Israel will be at peace

The king of the north "shalt say, I will go up to the land of unwalled villages; I will go to those who are at rest, who dwell safely, all of them dwelling without walls, and having neither bars nor gates" (v. 11). Israel will be at peace. That's precisely the nature of the first three-and-a-half years of the Tribulation. The Antichrist will become the protector of Israel by making a pact with them for seven years (Dan. 9:27). The resulting peace will cause Israel to lower its defenses in misplaced reliance on the power of the Antichrist.

(c) Israel will be in its latter days

"In the latter days" (Ezek. 38:16) is an eschatological expression that indicates the events described in Ezekiel 38 will take place during Israel's seventieth week (the Tribulation).

(d) Israel's enemy will be far north

Ezekiel 38:2 says, "Son of man, set thy face against Gog, of the land of Magog, the chief prince of Meshech and Tubal." Meshech and Tubal are the names of ancient peoples who lived in northern Mesopotamia and the Caucasus region of modern Russia. The people of the northern king are described as "Gomer, and all its hordes; the house of Togarmah of the north quarters . . . from the north parts" (Ezek. 38:6; 39:2). The Hebrew word translated "north" in those verses refers to the far north. The only country far north of Israel is Russia.

According to Ezekiel 38:5 when Russia attacks it will be joined by Persia (Iran), Cush (Ethiopia), and Put (Libya)—representatives of an Arab alliance that will chafe under the power of the Antichrist and the Western alliance. They will unite with Russia and attack his interests in the Middle East.

*b*) The chariots (v. 40*c*)

"[The king of the north will attack] with chariots, and with horsemen, and with many ships."

The king of the north will attack with the modern counterparts of chariots, horsemen, and ships—everything they've got. But according to Ezekiel 39 God will give victory to the Antichrist. Apparently five-sixths of the Russian army will be destroyed by supernatural intervention (vv. 2-5). Thus the Antichrist will win not by his own power but because God will exercise His power.

*c*) The conquest (vv. 40*d*-43)

(1) Of the Russians (v. 40*d*)

"[The Antichrist] shall enter into the countries, and shall overflow and pass through."

The Antichrist will decimate the forces of Russia and those confederated with it. Only one-sixth of the northern army will survive to retreat back to its land. This is history—though it hasn't happened yet, it will.

(2) Of the Arabs (v. 41)

"He shall enter also into the glorious land, and many countries shall be overthrown, but these shall escape out of his hand, even Edom, and Moab, and the chief of the children of Ammon."

After defeating the kings of the south and the north (the African army, the Russian army, and the Arab allies of Russia), the Antichrist will enter into Israel ("the glorious land"). He may wonder how he won since Ezekiel 38-39 indicates it's divine intervention that will destroy the northern and southern armies. After entering Israel the Antichrist's forces will devastate the southern territory (v. 42). But verse 41 indicates that Edom, Moab, and Ammon (to the southeast of Israel) will escape his depredations. That's because He will be busy to the southwest with the African army. He won't be concerned about the southeast because it is of minimal strategic value, being mostly desert. The angel's revelation to Daniel concerning the future was remarkably specific.

(3) Of the Africans (vv. 42-43)

"He shall stretch forth his hand also upon the countries, and the land of Egypt shall not escape. But he shall have power over the treasures of gold and of silver, and over all the precious things of Egypt; and the Libyans and the Ethiopians shall be at his steps."

By destroying both the Russian army and its Arab allies from the north, as well as the

African army from the south, the Antichrist will become the master of the world. He will thus pass the first great test of his ability to subdue revolution. It's at this time that he will truly begin to sense his power. He will destroy the false church and begin to persecute Israel. He'll call for the whole world to worship him and abolish all other religions. He'll set himself up as God, tolerating no other authority and ruling in absolute supremacy. All the allies of Russia will be "at his steps" (v. 43; lit., "in his train"), meaning they will follow him subserviently.

d) The cataclysm (v. 44)

"But tidings out of the east and out of the north shall trouble him; therefore, he shall go forth with great fury to destroy, and utterly to sweep away many."

At this point in the Tribulation the events described in Revelation 6-18 begin to unfold. God will pour out His wrath: the seven seals will be opened, the seven trumpets blown, and the seven bowls poured out. His wrath will engulf the earth while the Antichrist attempts to reign in God's place.

The one-sixth of the Russian army that God spares from destruction will regroup for a second attack on the Antichrist. The "tidings out of the east" (Dan. 11:44) are explained in Revelation 9:13-16: at the blowing of the sixth trumpet the apostle John "heard a voice from the four horns of the golden altar which is before God, saying to the sixth angel who had the trumpet, Loose the four angels who are bound in the great River, Euphrates. And the four angels were loosed, who were prepared for an hour, and a day, and a month, and a year, to slay the third part of men. And the number of the army of the horsemen were two hundred thousand."

That passage describes an army that will come from the east of Israel. It may be a demonic host or it may be a human army, perhaps from Communist China. Back in the May 22, 1965, edition of *Time* magazine (p. 35) it was reported that the Chinese standing militia numbers over 200 million—an army that has been ready for a long time and ironically knows little of the book of Revelation. The eastern army will move toward Israel, desiring to gain control over the Middle East and throw off the rule of the Antichrist.

According to Daniel 11:44 the Antichrist will triumph again in a second great battle. That's not surprising because he will have Satan on his side helping him.

e) The climax (v. 45a)

"He [the Antichrist] shall plant the tabernacle of his palace between the seas in the glorious holy mountain."

Mount Zion lies between the Mediterranean and Dead seas. In the Temple of Jerusalem the Antichrist will set up his base of operations and declare himself God. That will occur near the end of the Tribulation. Israel will lie devastated as a result of war and persecution. Two-thirds of the people of Israel will be killed (Zech. 13:8). But that is not the way history ends.

f) The condemnation (v. 45b)

"He shall come to his end, and none shall help him."

Just when he seems invincible the Antichrist will come to his end. When he thinks he has won the Battle of Armageddon the Lord Jesus Christ will descend with a sword from the sky and slay him (Rev. 19:11-21; 2 Thess. 2:8). The Antichrist will be no match for God's true King.

Just prior to Christ's return Israel will reach its deepest point of sorrow, suffering, and humiliation. As He comes to their rescue they will look upon Him "whom they have pierced" (Zech. 12:10), and they will be redeemed. They will already have been evangelized by the 144,000 and Jewish witnesses during the second three-and-a-half years of the Tribulation (Rev. 7:4-10). At their lowest point they will finally accept the gospel they have heard.

## Conclusion

There are three major lessons in the eleventh chapter of Daniel:

A. God Is in Control

Every detail of history is under God's control. Every ruler—Ahasuerus, Alexander, Antiochus the Great, Antiochus Epiphanes, the Antichrist, and anyone in between—has carried out His will. It's comforting to know that history is His story. All is in His hand, and there's no need to worry about the future.

B. God Is Purging His People

God continues to purge Israel. That purging will end in an incredible day of testing for Israel. In Luke 21:28 the Lord warns, "When these things begin to come to pass, then look up, and lift up your heads; for your redemption draweth near."

C. God Will Triumph over Evil

The world's godless system will end in a holocaust, and Christ will triumph over it. For those who know and love the Lord Jesus Christ that will inaugurate a blissful future that will last forever! I hope you know Him.

1. What does God use suffering to accomplish in the lives of His people (Dan. 11:35; see p. 94)?
2. How do some commentators view the events of Daniel 11:36-45 in the chronology of history? What do they refuse to accept (see p. 95)?
3. Why is it probable that Daniel 11:36-45 is speaking of the future (see pp. 95-96)?
4. List the titles in Scripture that describe the Antichrist (see p. 97).
5. Why will the Antichrist be able to do everything "according to his will"? Who will empower and cooperate with him (see p. 97)?
6. Why will it be necessary for the Western world under the Antichrist to step forward as the protector of Israel (see pp. 97-98)?
7. In what way will the Antichrist be the epitome of pride (see pp. 98-99)?
8. Although he will exalt himself above all, what will the Antichrist tolerate at first (see p. 99)?
9. Why will God tolerate the atrocities of the Antichrist? What will his blasphemy and oppression lead Israel to do (see p. 99)?
10. In what three ways will the Antichrist be perverted (Dan. 11:37; see pp. 100-101)?
11. Why may it be said that the world today is ready for a leader like the Antichrist (see p. 101)?
12. Instead of God or people, what will the Antichrist worship (Dan. 11:38; see pp. 101-102)?
13. How will the Antichrist convince people to recognize his authority and persuade them to be loyal to him (see p. 102)?
14. What will erupt against the Antichrist's world rule (Dan.11:40; see p. 103)?
15. Identify the country that the phrase "the king of the north" represents. What evidence exists to identify it (see pp. 103-104)?
16. Describe the conditions in Israel when the "king of the north" will attack (Ezek. 38:11; see p. 104).
17. What nations will help the "king of the north" in its attack on Israel (Ezek. 38:5; see p. 105)?
18. Whose power is responsible for the Antichrist's victory over the armies of the north and south (see p. 105)?

19. What will the Antichrist do after he defeats the northern and southern armies (Dan. 11:41; see pp. 106-107)?
20. What tidings from the east and north will trouble the Antichrist (Rev. 9:13-16; see pp. 107-108)?
21. Why isn't it surprising that the Antichrist will triumph in the second great battle predicted in Daniel 11:44 (see p. 108)?
22. When will the Antichrist finally meet his end? What will happen to Israel at that point (see pp. 108-109)?

### Pondering the Principles

1. God will tolerate the atrocities of the Antichrist because they will be part of the process of purifying Israel. It's the incredible blasphemy and oppression of the Antichrist that will finally bring Israel to recognize the Lord Jesus Christ as their Messiah. Meditate on Isaiah 1:24-26, Malachi 3:1-4, Ephesians 1:4, and 1 Peter 5:8-10. The purity of God's people is a priority in His plan. Are you working with God in purifying your life (cf. 1 John 3:3)? Are you sensitive to His leading and pliable to His correction? Or does it require extreme measures (as it has for Israel) for you to respond in accordance with His will?

2. It's a great comfort to know that God is in control of history. When Gog, the northern prince, brings his army out of the north to gain control of Israel, it will be supernaturally destroyed by God. Read through Ezekiel 38:18-39:7. God will be glorified by destroying forces that oppose Him and seek to destroy His people. At that time those who wondered about or denied God's existence will clearly see His power displayed (Ezek. 38:23). Though we don't see such massive demonstrations today, there are other miracles that are no less dramatic. Have you recently witnessed the transformation of someone who has received a spiritual birth through faith in Christ? That is no less a demonstration of God's sovereign power. Praise the Lord, who someday will be known by everyone for His great power and majesty (Rev. 15:3).

111

# 7

# The Great Tribulation—Part 1

**Outline**

Introduction
A. The Importance of Hope
B. The Intensity of the Coming Holocaust

Lesson
I. A Special Distress (v. 1*b*)
   A. The History of Israel's Suffering
   B. The Height of Israel's Suffering
      1. Matthew 24:7-22
      2. Revelation 6-18
      3. Jeremiah 30:4-7
      4. Zechariah 13:8-9
II. A Special Defender (v. 1*a*)
   A. He Protected the Messiah
   B. He Will Protect Israel
III. A Special Deliverance (v. 1*c*)
   A. Through the two witnesses
   B. Through the 144 thousand witnesses
IV. A Special Destiny (v. 2)
   A. Declared
      1. By Abraham
      2. By Job
      3. By Isaiah
      4. By Hosea
      5. By David
   B. Described
      1. Everlasting life
         *a*) Its synonyms
         *b*) Its sequence

# Introduction

A. The Importance of Hope

Next to faith and love the greatest reality in the world is hope (1 Cor. 13:13). Faith, hope, and love are the three most important elements in life because man cannot live without them.

Daniel 12 begins with a message of hope. Hope is what makes life meaningful. Without light at the end of a tunnel a man will despair. He must be able to anticipate great things in the future, or he will find himself unable to enjoy life now.

Hope is especially important to those who suffer. God knows that for a man to endure present stress he must have hope in a better future. That's why throughout the Bible God presents mankind a great and eternal hope for the future. It's a hope beyond all others, one that gives our present life full meaning.

Hope is what we find at the end of the book of Daniel. In preceding chapters the prophet received revelation of the disastrous future history of Israel. They reveal that the Gentile world powers of Babylon, Medo-Persia, Greece, and Rome would dominate Israel. And they were correct: Israel has been savagely abused and slaughtered throughout its history. But on a note of hope Daniel closes with the promise that Israel's oppression will end when their Messiah returns.

## B. The Intensity of the Coming Holocaust

The heart of Daniel's message is found in Daniel 11:35: the main purpose of Israel's chastening is "to test them, and to purge, and to make them white." God has given His people over to persecution until they are purified and respond properly to Him. But had God ended with a bleak message of suffering, there would have been no light at the end of the tunnel. Therefore in the first three verses of chapter 12 God gives Israel the light of hope. Though Israel's future would be a dark one for thousands of years—the people would refuse to respond to God, reject their own Messiah, and accept Satan's counterfeit (the Antichrist) in His place—at the end there is hope.

Daniel 12 introduces the hope that follows the terrible events predicted in Daniel 11:36-45. During that period the Antichrist will be the consummate oppressor of Israel. He will cause the greatest suffering the Jewish people have ever endured, slaughtering more of their own than Hitler ever did. But when that persecution is at its worst during the Great Tribulation, hope will dawn. Though "the time of Jacob's trouble" (Jer. 30:7) will be dominated by the Antichrist and he will cause the massive war that will end in Armageddon, once he desecrates the Temple and attempts to slaughter the entire nation of Israel, the events at the opening of chapter 12 will unfold.

The last half of the Tribulation will be marked by the wars of the Antichrist. He will fight against armies from the north, south, and east of Israel, and will win great victories. By those victories he will establish his absolute power over the earth. At the height of his power he will commit an abominable deed in the Temple by establishing himself as the only God. In spite of those terrible future events the angel told Daniel that when things were at their worst it would nearly be time for things to become their best. The darkest hour would come just before the dawn.

Lesson

## I. A SPECIAL DISTRESS (v. 1b)

"At that time . . . there shall be a time of trouble, such as never was since there was a nation even to that same time."

### A. The History of Israel's Suffering

The angel revealed to Daniel the coming of a time of unprecedented distress. In the past Israel suffered under the Babylonians, Medo-Persians, Greeks, and Romans. They suffered after the Roman era at the hands of Crusaders and various European leaders, culminating with Adolf Hitler. They have suffered since that time. All that suffering has served as God's disciplining rod. Their sufferings are designed to purge their rebellion and rejection, leading them to turn back to God in faith. But the worst suffering is yet to come.

### B. The Height of Israel's Suffering

The phrase "a time of trouble, such as never was" is a Hebrew idiomatic expression that means the time of trouble referred to will be the worst ever (cf. Ex. 9:18, 24). Things aren't going to get better for Israel—they'll get worse. Similar affirmations are found elsewhere in Scripture.

1. Matthew 24:7-22—Jesus said concerning the Tribulation and the activities of the Antichrist, "Nation shall rise against nation, and kingdom against kingdom; and there shall be famines, and pestilences, and earthquakes, in various places. All these are the beginning of sorrows. . . . When ye, therefore, shall see the abomination of desolation, spoken of by Daniel the prophet, stand in the holy place (whosoever readeth, let him understand), then let them who are in Judea flee into the mountains; let him who is on the housetop not come down to take anything out of his house; neither let him who is in the field return back to take his clothes. And woe unto those

who are with child, and to those who nurse children in those days! But pray that your flight be not in the winter, neither on the sabbath day; for then shall be great tribulation, such as was not since the beginning of the world to this time, no, nor ever shall be. And except those days should be shortened, there should no flesh be saved." Jesus' warning reiterated the revelation Daniel heard: there would be a future time of unprecedented trouble for God's people Israel.

2. Revelation 6-18—The book of Revelation describes the incredible final events of human history. Chapters 6-18 present the details of the last three-and-a-half years of Daniel's seventieth week (Dan. 9:24-27) —the Great Tribulation. The apostle John saw in a vision several terrifying elements belonging to that period: war (Rev. 6:3-4), famine (6:5-6), the death of 25 percent of the world's population (6:7-8), the collapse of the heavenly bodies (6:12-14), the destruction of one-third of land and sea—together with what they contained—(8:7-9), the pollution of one-third of earth's fresh water and the death of those who drink from it (8:10-11), the destruction of one-third of the sun, moon, and stars (8:12), the release of hell's demons to overrun the earth (9:1-11), the slaughter initiated by the beast and his false prophet during their vile administration (13:7, 15), the affliction of painful body sores (16:2), the death of all remaining creatures in the sea (16:3), further pollution of fresh water (16:4), scorching sunlight (16:9), and darkness (16:10). More demons and judgments of wrath will afflict the living until Christ's return as described in Revelation 19. In addition God will allow the Antichrist to oppress Israel in a final act of purging. The Tribulation will be an incredible time of suffering when God's judgments occur simultaneously with Satan's persecutions in a historical apex of misery. It will be especially difficult for the people of Israel.

3. Jeremiah 30:4-7—"These are the words that the Lord spoke concerning Israel and concerning Judah. For

thus saith the Lord, We have heard a voice of trembling, of fear, and not of peace. Ask now, and see whether a man doth travail with child? Why do I see every man with his hands on his loins, like a woman in travail, and all faces are turned into paleness? Alas! for that day is great, so that none is like it; it is even the time of Jacob's trouble." During the Tribulation mankind will experience agony like the excruciating pain of childbirth.

4. Zechariah 13:8-9—"It shall come to pass that in all the land, saith the Lord, two parts in it shall be cut off and die; but the third shall be left in it. And I will bring the third part through the fire, and will refine them as silver is refined, and will test them as gold is tested; they shall call on my name, and I will hear them. I will say, It is my people; and they shall say, The Lord is my God." During the Tribulation two-thirds of the Jewish people will die, but the other third will be redeemed. Israel's rebelliousness will be purged away, and they will believe in Christ.

Israel's future contains a time of distress without a historical equal. It's known as the time of Jacob's trouble, the seventieth week of Daniel, or the Great Tribulation. Yet during that time Israel will receive unique assistance.

II.   A SPECIAL DEFENDER (v. 1a)

"At that time shall Michael stand up, the great prince who standeth for the children of thy people."

Israel will not be completely destroyed because the archangel Michael will undertake their defense. He may be the most powerful of all angelic creatures. Throughout Israel's history his responsibility has been to defend God's people. In both the Old and New Testaments he is described as the leader of the holy angels.

Jude 9 tells us that Michael fought with Satan over the body of Moses. His care for God's people extends to not permitting the desecration of their dead bodies. Daniel 10 says that when demons tried to stop an angel from delivering his message to Daniel, the angel called to Michael for help. The angel told Daniel, "Michael, one of the chief princes, came to help me. . . . There is none that holdeth with me in these things, but Michael, your prince" (vv. 13, 21). Since God assigned Michael the task of caring for Israel, it's not surprising for him to appear in their greatest distress. At the time of the most furious persecution and oppression, Michael will come to the rescue.

Michael will rescue God's people by directly countering Satan's activities. During the Tribulation Satan will release hell's forces against Israel. His intent will be the complete destruction of the nation—a goal he tried to accomplish previously so that the Messiah would be prevented from coming to establish His kingdom. Revelation 12 describes how in the end times a great battle will occur as all the demons of hell pursue the nation of Israel.

## A. He Protected the Messiah

"There appeared a great wonder in heaven—a woman [Israel] clothed with the sun, and the moon under her feet, and upon her head a crown of twelve stars" (Rev. 12:1). That pictures the twelve tribes of Israel in prophetic imagery. "She, being with child, cried, travailing in birth, and pained to be delivered. . . . And she brought forth a male child, who was to rule all nations with a rod of iron; and her child was caught up unto God, and to his throne" (vv. 2-5). That describes the birth of Christ (the Messiah) and His ascension into heaven. Then "the woman fled into the wilderness" (v. 6). Israel fled because "there appeared another wonder in heaven; and, behold, a great red dragon, having seven heads and ten horns, and seven crowns upon his heads. And his tail drew the third part of the stars of heaven and did cast them to the earth; and the dragon stood before the woman who was ready to be delivered, to devour her child as soon as it was born" (vv. 3-4). Satan is described as a dragon that embodies all Gentile governments in the final form of the Roman Empire. When he rebelled against God he apparently took one-third of the angels with him—they became demons. Although his

119

force is not as large as God's, it has proven to be very powerful.

Nevertheless, righteous power always overcomes evil power. Satan unsuccessfully tried to prevent the birth of the Messiah. After the Christ Child was born he worked through Herod in an attempt to "devour" that Child. Throughout Jesus' life Satan tried to kill Him. When Christ ascended to God's throne, Satan attacked Christ's followers. During the Tribulation Satan, the demons, and the beast (the Antichrist) will attack Israel again. But Israel will flee "into the wilderness, where she hath a place prepared by God, that they should feed her there a thousand two hundred and threescore days" (v. 6).

B. He Will Protect Israel

During the Tribulation's second three-and-a-half years God will protect Israel by the power of Michael. The demons will desire to overrun the earth and destroy Israel, but Michael and the holy angels will war against them in heaven: "There was war in heaven; Michael and his angels fought against the dragon, and the dragon fought and his angels, and prevailed not, neither was their place found any more in heaven. And the great dragon was cast out, that old serpent, called the Devil and Satan, who deceiveth the whole world; he was cast out into the earth, and his angels were cast out with him" (vv. 7-9). I believe the demons will lose some of their supernatural power at that point: "I heard a loud voice saying in heaven, Now is come salvation, and strength, and the kingdom of our God, and the power of his Christ; for the accuser of our brethren is cast down, who accused them before our God day and night. And they overcame him by the blood of the Lamb, and by the word of their testimony; and they loved not their lives unto the death. Therefore rejoice, ye heavens, and ye that dwell in them. Woe to the inhabiters of the earth and of the sea! For the devil is come down unto you, having great wrath, because he knoweth that he hath but a short time" (vv. 10-12).

Satan's plan to ruin Israel will be thwarted. In the short time that he has left he will apparently overrun the earth with evil. But he will be unsuccessful in his attempt to destroy Israel because he will have already lost the battle: "When the dragon saw that he was cast unto the earth, he persecuted the woman [Israel] who brought forth the male child. And to the woman were given two wings of a great eagle, that she might fly into the wilderness, into her place, where she is nourished for a time, and times, and half a time [three-and-a-half years], from the face of the serpent. And the serpent cast out of his mouth water like a flood after the woman, that he might cause her to be carried away by the flood. And the earth helped the woman, and the earth opened her mouth and swallowed up the flood which the dragon cast out of his mouth" (vv. 13-16). The opening of the earth may be a repeat of what happened to Korah, Dathan, and Abiram in the Old Testament (Num. 16:31-33). In this case it will be the beast and all his army who will be swallowed up.

Satan will then intensify his efforts to destroy the Jewish remnant: "The dragon was angry with the woman, and went to make war with the remnant of her seed, who keep the commandments of God, and have the testimony of Jesus Christ" (v. 17). Though persecution will continue after Michael's defeat of Satan, that defeat is the turning point toward victory for Israel. That's because Satan will then no longer be "the prince of the power of the air" (Eph. 2:2) after he is cast to the earth. Though the major battle will be won, he will continue to seek Israel's destruction for a short time. But Michael, their special defender, will protect them for the second half of the Tribulation. It is significant that the angelic messenger in Daniel 10 revealed Michael's power over Satan and his responsibility to protect Israel. That gave Daniel confidence—he knew Michael would be present at the time of Israel's greatest need.

## III. A SPECIAL DELIVERANCE (v. 1c)

"At that time thy people shall be delivered."

Romans 11:26 declares, "All Israel shall be saved; as it is written, There shall come out of Zion the Deliverer" (cf. Isa. 59:20). "Alas! for that day is great, so that none is like it, it is even the time of Jacob's trouble, but he shall be saved out of it. . . . For I am with thee, saith the Lord, to save thee. . . . For I will restore health unto thee, and I will heal thee of thy wounds" (Jer. 30:7-17). At the time Israel is delivered it will also be redeemed.

What part of Israel will be saved? In the end times apostates and rebels will be purged out of Israel. Only those remaining will be protected. Zechariah 13:8 says two-thirds of Israel will die. The one-third left constitutes the godly remnant to whom the promise of redemption belongs. The end of Daniel 12:1 verifies that fact: the delivered are "every one that shall be found written in the book." The promise of deliverance and salvation is for those who believe.

The book of Revelation explains how the remnant of Israel will come to believe in Jesus Christ—the One Judaism has so long rejected.

### A. Through the Two Witnesses

According to Revelation 11 God will set apart two witnesses with miraculous powers. They are described as two olive branches in verse 4. After the Antichrist kills them their bodies will be viewed worldwide—perhaps by use of satellite television (v. 9). They will be murdered because of the prophetic message they will preach. The world will rejoice at their death. But after three-and-a-half days they will rise from the dead. I imagine their message will become more convincing at that point!

### B. Through the 144,000 Witnesses

Revelation 7 and 14 reveal that 144,000 Jewish people will be sealed and protected by God to serve as evangelists during the Tribulation: 12,000 from each of Israel's tribes. Their ministry will be essentially the same as that of the two witnesses: leading Jewish people to faith in their Messiah. Those who believe will in turn reach others— even in the midst of that holocaust! In that way a living remnant will be preserved as a redeemed nation. God assured Israel through Jeremiah, "I am with thee; for I will make a full end of all the nations to which I have driven thee; but I will not make a full end of thee" (46:28).

Though deliverance of Israel will involve the personal salvation of individuals, it will occur on a scale large enough to be termed a national deliverance. The remnant of believing Jews during the tribulation constitutes the "all Israel" of Romans 11:26. Thus Israel's hope is that someday its purging will end, the nation will be saved, and the long-awaited messianic kingdom will be established.

## IV. A SPECIAL DESTINY (v. 2)

"Many of those who sleep in the dust of the earth shall awake, some to everlasting life, and some to shame and everlasting contempt."

### A. Declared

Resurrection will be the climax of the Tribulation. Some commentators think the Jewish people never had the hope of the resurrection because they didn't have a clear understanding of life after death. But that's not what Scripture shows.

#### 1. By Abraham

According to Hebrews 11:19 Abraham willingly offered his son Isaac because he was confident of the resurrection of the dead.

## 2. By Job

Job, who may have penned the oldest book in the Bible (he probably lived before Moses), cherished the hope of resurrection. He said, "I know that my redeemer liveth, and that he shall stand at the latter day upon the earth; and though after my skin worms destroy this body, yet in my flesh shall I see God, whom I shall see for myself, and mine eyes shall behold, and not another, though my heart be consumed within me" (19:25-27).

## 3. By Isaiah

Isaiah, who lived more than a century before Daniel, predicted that dead men would live again and their bodies rise from the dead (26:19).

## 4. By Hosea

Through Hosea, a contemporary of Isaiah, the Lord said, "I will ransom [Israel] from the power of Sheol; I will redeem them from death" (13:14).

## 5. By David

David was predicting the resurrection of Christ when he wrote, "My flesh also shall rest in hope. For Thou wilt not leave my soul in sheol, neither wilt thou permit thine Holy One to see corruption" (Ps. 16:9-10).

The resurrection has been the hope of God's people from the beginning. The angel's message to Daniel was good reason for hope: Israel will be saved, and the resurrection will indeed occur.

## B. Described

Daniel 12 and Revelation 20 speak of two aspects to the resurrection: one is to "everlasting life" whereas the other is to "shame and everlasting contempt." Both the positive and negative parts to the resurrection involve the resurrection of the body.

1. Everlasting life

   a) Its synonyms

   The resurrection to everlasting life is a resurrection of the just (Acts 24:15). John 5:29 calls it "the resurrection of life;" Hebrews 11:35 terms it "a better resurrection." It's the resurrection of all glorified saints: all believers from the Old and New Testament eras, as well as from the Tribulation period, will enjoy everlasting life.

   b) Its sequence

   The "first resurrection" (Rev. 20:5) has three parts.

   (1) Christ

   The first resurrection began with Christ. He was "the first fruits of them that slept" (1 Cor. 15:20). After He was raised from the dead, several others were raised with Him (Matt. 27:52-53). That initial resurrection was a picture of what will happen in the coming kingdom.

   (2) The church

   The second part of this first resurrection involves the church. That will take place at the rapture, according to 1 Thessalonians 4:16-17: "The dead in Christ shall rise first; then we who are alive and remain shall be caught up together with them in the clouds, to meet the Lord in the air; and so shall we ever be with the Lord."

### (3) The Old Testament and Tribulation saints

The Tribulation will occur after the church is removed from the earth—the church wasn't in Israel's first sixty-nine weeks, and it will not be in its seventieth week (cf. Dan. 9:24-27). During that final week of seven years God will deal exclusively with Israel. At the end of that time of purging, the third and final part of the first resurrection will take place: the raising of the Old Testament and Tribulation saints (cf. Dan. 12:13; Rev. 6:9-11). It will include Gentiles who were saved and martyred during the Tribulation (Rev. 7:9-10).

In Revelation 20:4 the apostle John gives a description of the first resurrection: "I saw thrones, and they sat upon them, and judgment was given unto them; and I saw the souls of them that were beheaded for the witness of Jesus, and for the word of God, and who had not worshiped the beast, neither his image, neither had received his mark upon their foreheads, or in their hands; and they lived and reigned with Christ a thousand years." That verse implies a resurrection. In his vision John saw the thousand-year millennial kingdom, where the saints of all the ages will be alive and reigning with Christ. Verses 5-6 say, "But the rest of the dead lived not again until the thousand years were finished. This is the first resurrection [prior to the thousand years]. Blessed and holy is he that hath part in the first resurrection."

2. Shame and everlasting contempt

The second resurrection has just one part. It will happen at the end of the Millennium, when God raises the bodies of the unjust from the dead. Revelation 20:7 provides the time frame: "When the thousand years are ended." Verses 11-15 provide some of its details: "I saw a great white throne, and him that sat on it. . . . And I saw the dead, small and great, stand before God, and the books were opened; and another book was opened, which is the book of life. And the dead were judged out of those things which were written in the books, according to their works. And the sea gave up the dead that were in it, and death and hades delivered up the dead that were in them; and they were judged every man according to their works. And death and hades were cast into the lake of fire. This is the second death. And whosoever was not found written in the book of life was cast into the lake of fire."

Daniel did not see the thousand-year gap between the two resurrections. In the Old Testament you'll find gaps in the flow of redemptive history. Peter said the prophets examined what they wrote in an attempt to understand what it meant, because they didn't have the full range of revelation (1 Pet. 1:10-11). Revelation 20 clarifies that the resurrection to life and the resurrection to shame and contempt will occur a thousand years apart. But prior to the New Testament clarification, the Jewish people didn't understand fully the timing of the resurrections.

Early in His ministry Jesus spoke of the two resurrections: "Marvel not at this; for the hour is coming, in which all that are in the graves shall hear [My] voice, and shall come forth: they that have done good, unto the resurrection of life; and they that have done evil, unto the resurrection of damnation" (John 5:28-29). All who have ever lived will be resurrected: some to life and some to death. The angel told Daniel that the resurrection is the hope of Israel.

V.   A SPECIAL DIVIDEND (v. 3)

"They that be wise shall shine like the brightness of the firmament; and they that turn many to righteousness, as the stars forever and ever."

Daniel 12:3 does not speak further about the punishment of the wicked since that event will occur a thousand years after the resurrection of the just. Verse 3 focuses on Israel's hope of the resurrection to everlasting life.

## A. The Recipients

At this resurrection will come reward—a time of special dividends. Those who will receive them are identified as "they that be wise." They will believe in Christ and remain faithful to Him through the time of their nation's purging. The wisest people in the world are the saved, and the biggest fools are the unsaved. Both Jews as well as Gentiles will come to faith in Christ during the Tribulation period. Revelation 7:9-10 says innumerable Gentiles will be saved during the Tribulation.

## B. The Rewards

### 1. Analyzed

Those who are rewarded "shall shine like the brightness of the firmament . . . as the stars forever and ever." I believe that means we will be rewarded in eternity by a capacity to manifest the blazing glory of God. When we look into the night sky we see stars of varying size and brilliance, but they are all beautiful. That's the way we will be in heaven. I believe our size and brightness depend on our faithfulness. All who know Jesus Christ will have the capacity to eternally radiate the glory of God, but those who "turn many to righteousness" will be especially bright.

According to the New Testament the rewards or crowns we will receive when we go to heaven will simply be ways of expressing our capacity to radiate the glory of God. If we're saved we'll shine like stars, and all the more if we've turned "many to righteousness." The brightest glories are reserved for those who have influenced others to believe in Christ. Thus the angel was telling Daniel that during the Tribulation Israel will be saved and lead others to Christ, including many Gentiles, "which no man could number, of all nations, and kindreds, and peoples, and tongues" (Rev. 7:9). The Jewish evangelists of the Tribulation will be able to manifest God's glory with a special brilliance.

## 2. Applied

We as Christians can apply that reward to ourselves. Our faithfulness to witness will help determine our eternal capacity to manifest the glory of God. We will shine like "stars" (v. 3). There have been many earthly stars in the past, such as Caesar, Napoleon, and Hitler, who have led great armies that wreaked havoc. There are also many contemporary stars. A walk down Hollywood Boulevard will reveal who they are right underneath your feet. But few earthly stars shine very long or brightly in the memory.

In contrast to the stars of earth the greatest stars in God's sky are those who "turn many to righteousness." One such star is John the Baptist. An angel said of him, "He shall be great in the sight of the Lord, and shall drink neither wine nor strong drink; and he shall be filled with the Holy Spirit, even from his mother's womb. And many of the children of Israel shall he turn to the Lord, their God" (Luke 1:15-16). Jesus said that John was the greatest human being who ever lived up to His time (Matt. 11:11). He will shine brightly forever when he is resurrected, with a tremendous capacity to radiate God's eternal glory because he turned "many to righteousness."

When you examine your own life, what have you done to contribute to such a future? Although the angel spoke specifically to Israel in Daniel 12, the principle extends to us. The Lord wants us all to be faithful to preach the Word and communicate the gospel. The apostle Paul wrote that we are to "be blameless and harmless, children of God, without rebuke, in the midst of a crooked and perverse nation, among whom [we] shine as lights in the world, holding forth the word of life" (Phil. 2:15-16).

# Conclusion

Daniel 12:1-3 is a message of hope. Israel can anticipate great distress in the future, yet they will be specially defended and delivered. All who are saved can look forward to a special destiny with glorious dividends: the capacity to radiate the glory of God forever. Israel's hope is ours as well: we are blessed in the tents of Shem (the Gentile descendants of Japheth will be spiritually blessed through the Jewish descendants of Shem—Gen. 9:27; 12:3). We become the seed of Abraham by faith, and therefore we too will reign in the kingdom and share the same privilege of radiating the glory of God!

## Focusing on the Facts

1. Why is hope essential to a meaningful life? Why is it especially important to those who suffer (see p. 114)?
2. What does God give Israel in the first three verses of Daniel 12? Why (see p. 115)?
3. When will hope dawn for Israel (see p. 115)?
4. What are Israel's sufferings designed to do (see p. 116)?
5. When will the unprecedented time of trouble for God's people occur (see p. 117)?
6. According to Zechariah 13:8 what portion of the Jewish people will be redeemed after their final purging (see p. 118)?
7. Who is the special defender that will stand up for Israel? What singular responsibility has he been given (see p. 118)?
8. Why has Satan continually tried to destroy the nation of Israel (see p. 119)?
9. How will demons be prevented from totally destroying Israel (see p. 120)?
10. What gave Daniel confidence (see p. 121)?
11. What part of Israel referred to in Romans 11:26 will be saved (see p. 122)?
12. How will the remnant of Israel come to believe in Jesus Christ (see pp. 122-123)?
13. Show from Scripture that the resurrection has always been the hope of God's people (see pp. 123-124).

14. Describe the three sequential parts of the first resurrection to everlasting life (see pp. 125-126).
15. According to Revelation 20:4, what will the saints of all ages do during the Millennium (see p. 126)?
16. What is the second resurrection? When will it occur (see p. 126)?
17. Who will receive special dividends at the resurrection (see p. 128)?
18. What will increase the brilliance of one's reward? Why will the Jewish evangelists of the Tribulation be able to brightly manifest God's glory (see pp. 128-129)?
19. What is one reason that John the Baptist was "great in the sight of the Lord" (Luke 1:15-16; see p. 129)?

## Pondering the Principles

1. What is your greatest hope? The Bible says that a Christian's greatest hope is the assurance that he will share in the glory of God (Rom. 5:2). Meditate on Romans 5:1-5. Why can we rejoice in the tribulations we face (vv. 3-4)? Our trials are like the rigors an athlete must endure while he trains. His hope to win is strengthened by the assurance that his suffering is a necessary part of the prize he will win. Do you rejoice in your trials, knowing that they are enhancing your spiritual maturity (James 1:2-4)? Christians in the midst of trials and suffering experience a hope and confidence in the future that will not disappoint them. Remember and take comfort in that hope as you face difficulties in your own life.

2. Are you committed to turning "many to righteousness" (Dan. 12:3)? If you desire to "be great in the sight of the Lord" (Luke 1:15), pray that you will be effectively used by God to speak about spiritual things to unbelievers. As you shine as a light "in the world, holding forth the word of life" (Phil. 2:15), look forward to the ability to manifest God's glory more fully in His presence in heaven.

# 8
# The Great Tribulation—Part 2

## Outline

Introduction

Review

Lesson
I. The Closing of Revelation (v. 4)
  A. For Preservation (v. 4a)
  B. For Future Study (v. 4b)
II. The Chronology of the Great Tribulation (vv. 5-7)
  A. The Question (vv. 5-6)
  B. The Answer (v. 7)
III. The Confusion of Daniel (vv. 8-9)
  A. Daniel's Inquiry (v. 8)
  B. The Lord's Reply (v. 9)
IV. The Cleansing of Israel (vv. 10-12)
  A. The Salvation of the Jewish Remnant (v. 10a)
  B. The Plight of the Wicked (v. 10b)
  C. The Establishment of the Kingdom (vv. 11-12)
    1. Through divine judgment (v. 11)
    2. Through preliminary preparation (v. 12)
V. The Commending of Daniel (v. 13)
  A. His Responsibility (v. 13a)
  B. His Resurrection (v. 13b)
  C. His Reward (v. 13c)

Conclusion

# Introduction

— In the last part of chapter 12 the Lord reveals the answers to some questions asked by Daniel and two angels. Daniel and the angels wanted to know the details of what would be coming to pass. Even with all the information already revealed in the book, much was still unknown about end-time events. The revelation they received so far piqued their interest to seek more answers. So in this closing section the Lord clarifies some final features about the end times. Some things about the future still remain a mystery. But let's look at what's been revealed to us.

## Review

During the Great Tribulation the Antichrist will severely oppress the nation of Israel (Dan. 12:1; see pp. 114-123). But in the midst of such persecution Israel will have the hope of the resurrection. At the end of the Tribulation will be the bodily resurrection of the righteous, and at the end of the Millennium that of the unrighteous. Some will be resurrected to eternal life, but others to eternal death (12:2; see pp. 123-127).

Israel will also have the hope of redemption, as God saves a remnant of the people in the midst of purging the nation. God's people will radiate His glory and influence many to trust Christ (12:3; see pp. 127-130).

## Lesson

I. THE CLOSING OF REVELATION (v. 4)

A. For Preservation (v. 4a)

"O Daniel, shut up the words, and seal the book, even to the time of the end."

The Hebrew phrase translated "shut up the words" speaks of preservation. "Book" refers to written material. The angel was telling Daniel that he had received the final words of this last revelation, covering Israel's history from Daniel's time to that of the Antichrist. Since Daniel would receive no further revelation, it was time to roll up the scroll and close it. Sealing the book would ensure the security of its contents and could even apply to an authenticating stamp so that people might treat it with respect. The revelation was to be preserved until "the time of the end," referring to the time of the Great Tribulation.

## When Will the Book of Daniel Be Fully Understood?

Daniel was told to preserve the divine messages given him until the time of the Great Tribulation. However, that doesn't mean the messages are hidden from us, only that they are safely preserved for those who come later—especially those living in the Great Tribulation. Today we obviously aren't in the Great Tribulation, but we can read and study the book of Daniel for ourselves. It's likely we can understand it better than Daniel did because we know the intervening history and have the book of Revelation and our Lord's commentary in Matthew 24-25.

But the fullest understanding of Daniel will not come until the Great Tribulation. During that time, the book of Daniel will undoubtedly be reopened and studied again by God's people. When they do so, they'll understand it as clearly as if they were reading the daily newspaper because all the events it foretells will come to pass. Many will believe in Christ not only as a result of the ministry of the 144,000 Jewish evangelists (Rev. 7:9-10), but also because the books of Daniel and Revelation chronicle the details of every Tribulation event.

B. For Future Study (v. 4b)

"Many shall run to and fro, and knowledge shall be increased."

In the Old Testament the Hebrew phrase "run to and fro" refers to someone's running around in search of something, especially information. For example, Jeremiah 5:1 says, "Run to and fro through the streets of Jerusalem, and see now, and know, and seek in its broad

places, if ye can find a man, if there be any that execut-
eth justice, that seeketh the truth; and I will pardon it."

Similarly, in the end times the Jewish people will want
to find an explanation for the unfolding events. They
will engage in a painstaking pursuit. And when they
come to the book of Daniel, their knowledge will be
increased because they'll understand the reason for their
suffering.

Bible teacher Leon Wood paraphrases the verse like this:
"Many shall run to and fro in their desire for knowledge of the last things, and, finding it in Daniel's book,
because it will have been preserved to this end, their
knowledge shall be increased" (*A Commentary on Daniel*
[Grand Rapids: Zondervan, 1973], p. 321). Daniel was to
preserve his book so that people of all time—from his day
until the end—could have knowledge of the events it
foretells.

## A Far-Reaching Impact

Daniel 12:3 says that those who are "wise shall shine like the
brightness of the firmament; and they that turn many to righteousness, as the stars forever and ever." The Lord will use Daniel to
turn many to righteousness—even millennia after his death—because he is the human author of the book that provides answers
about the Tribulation.

So the angel was saying to Daniel, "The content of the
prophecy is sealed. At this present time any attempt to
fully understand the future will be impossible, but in
the end it will all become clear." The obvious question
is, When will the end be? Undoubtedly Daniel wanted
to ask that question because he asks a similar one later
in the chapter (v. 8). But before he could do so, two
angels asked first.

## II. THE CHRONOLOGY OF THE GREAT TRIBULATION (vv. 5-7)

### A. The Question (vv. 5-6)

"Then I, Daniel, looked and, behold, there stood two others, the one on this side of the bank of the river, and the other on that side of the bank of the river. And one said to the man clothed in linen, who was above the waters of the river, How long shall it be to the end of these wonders?"

According to Daniel 10:4, Daniel was near the river Hiddekel, the Hebrew name for the Tigris River. Looking toward that river, Daniel saw two figures—apparently angels—in addition to the one already speaking to him. Perhaps the two came as witnesses to confirm the revelation about to be made.

The two were just as curious as Daniel about future events. Apparently angels don't know all the details about end-time events either. That's not surprising since Christ said no person or angel knows when the events preceding His coming will occur, but only the Father (Matt. 24:36). Even Christ in His human state didn't know (Mark 13:32). And the apostle Peter pointed out that angels are curious even about the nature of salvation (1 Pet. 1:12). Possibly being as fascinated by prophecy as we are, the angels asked their question before Daniel could.

Daniel saw a man clothed in linen positioned over the river. Chapter 10 helps identify that Person: "In the four and twentieth day of the first month, as I was by the side of the great river, which is Hiddekel, then I lifted up mine eyes, and looked, and, behold, a certain man clothed in linen, whose loins were girded with fine gold of Uphaz; his body also was like the beryl, and his face like the appearance of lightning, and his eyes like lamps of fire, and his arms and his feet in color like to polished bronze, and the voice of his words like the voice of a multitude" (vv. 4-6; cf. Rev. 1:13-16).

The man clothed in fine linen was the preincarnate Christ. That's evident because the angels were asking Him for information they didn't have. Furthermore, the angels were in a subordinate position by the edge of the river, while the One in linen was elevated "above the waters of the river" (Dan. 12:6). He was clothed in linen because that was the garment of the priesthood, its white color symbolizing holiness and purity.

The angels asked, "How long shall it be to the end of these wonders?" (12:6). They wanted to know about the "wonders" connected with the reign of the Antichrist. Their question was not concerned with the entire history from Daniel's day to that of the Antichrist but only with the conclusion of events. The angels wanted to know when the Antichrist would be permitted to bring oppressive measures against Israel and how long that oppression would last.

Why did the angels make such an inquiry? Perhaps even back in Daniel's time they were tired of fighting demons. They probably longed for the battle to be over. The archangel Michael had been defending the people of Israel for a long time. Surely he and his angelic army are just as anxious to see redemption completed as you and I are today.

The angels asked their question even though they had already received a satisfactory answer. It had been revealed that the Great Tribulation would last three-and-a-half years, and that it would occur long in the future (e.g., 7:25). Maybe they needed an affirmation. Or maybe they posed the question, already knowing the answer, that it might be reinforced for Daniel's sake.

B. The Answer (v. 7)

"I heard the man clothed in linen, who was above the waters of the river, when he held up his right hand and his left hand unto heaven, and swore by him who liveth forever, that it shall be for a time, times, and a half, and when he shall have accomplished the breaking up of the power of the holy people, all these things shall be finished."

Whenever a Jewish person would make an oath, he raised his right hand. We do that today when a person testifies in court, raising his right hand and promising to tell the truth. That Christ raised both His hands emphasizes the announcement of an absolutely binding affirmation. He swore by His Father, "who liveth forever" (cf. 1 Tim. 6:16).

The Hebrew phrase translated "a time, times, and a half" time means that the Antichrist's reign of terror will last three-and-a-half years (cf. 7:25). The Lord described the activity of the Antichrist as "the breaking up of the power of the holy people." The Tribulation is divinely designed to devastate Israel, a nation set apart unto God. When the Antichrist comes, the people of Israel will place their trust in him and sign an allegiance with him for seven years (9:27).

However, in the middle of that period, he will turn against them and break their power. His persecution against them will be unprecedented in history (Dan. 12:1). The Lord's intention is not to destroy His people, but to bring them to the point of brokenness so they will look to their Messiah,-"whom they have pierced, and they shall mourn for him, as one mourneth for his only son" (Zech. 12:10). Having nowhere to flee but into the loving arms of Christ after three-and-a-half years of relentless persecution, Israel will accept Him as their Savior and Lord.

The book of Revelation affirms that the duration of Israel's intense persecution will be three-and-a-half years:

1. Revelation 11:3—The Lord said, "I will give power unto my two witnesses, and they shall prophesy a thousand two hundred and threescore days." Those 1,260 days are the equivalent of three-and-a-half years based on a thirty-day-month Jewish calendar.

2. Revelation 12:6—God will protect the remnant of believing Israel for "a thousand two hundred and threescore days."

3. Revelation 12:14—Israel will be "nourished for a time, and times, and half a time."

4. Revelation 13:5—"Power was given unto [the Antichrist] to continue forty and two months."

It will be near history's end when the Antichrist crushes "the holy people" (Dan. 12:7). Then they will in truth be holy. That's because their sin will be so deep and their destruction so complete that they will look to their covenant-keeping God. He will be faithful to redeem them through the Messiah. Indeed there will be a glorious salvation for Israel in the future!

III. THE CONFUSION OF DANIEL (vv. 8-9)

Having heard the answer to the angels' question, Daniel was still confused. Keep in mind that he didn't have the insight of further revelation and history we do today.

A. Daniel's Inquiry (v. 8)

"I heard, but I understood not. Then said I, O my Lord, what shall be the end of these things?"

The tense of the Hebrew verb translated "understood" indicates that Daniel struggled to understand what had been said, but that understanding escaped him. Whereas the angels asked about the time and length of the persecution, Daniel was more concerned about what kind of persecution his people would suffer. He knew Israel's affliction would be catastrophic, but he wanted specific detail about events that would take place. For instance, how severely would his people suffer before turning to the Messiah?

B. The Lord's Reply (v. 9)

> "And he said, Go thy way, Daniel; for the words are closed up and sealed till the time of the end."

That was intended not only as mild rebuke, but also to bring comfort. Daniel didn't need to worry because God was in control and the events were far in the future from Daniel's standpoint. The revelation Daniel received will be preserved for God's people in the future and be a source of knowledge, comfort, and salvation to them. So the Lord was telling Daniel to be content with what He had revealed, staying away from useless speculation.

Today many people are trying to figure out every detail in prophecy, but that often adds unnecessary confusion. Let's accept what God has revealed, but not try to go any further. We don't have to catalog every prophetic detail and fully explain its meaning. Sometimes we must learn to say, "I just don't know." That's not necessarily a sign of weakness, but can be evidence of trusting in God.

IV. THE CLEANSING OF ISRAEL (vv. 10-12)

A. The Salvation of the Jewish Remnant (v. 10a)

> "Many shall be purified, and made white, and tested."

Born out of this time of testing will be a redeemed remnant of Jewish people who will turn in faith to their Messiah (cf. Dan. 11:35). Zechariah 13 says, "It shall come to pass that in all the land, saith the Lord, two parts in it shall be cut off and die; but the third shall be left in it. And I will bring the third part through the fire, and will refine them as silver is refined, and will test them as gold is tested; they shall call on my name, and I will hear them. I will say, It is my people; and they shall say, The Lord is my God" (vv. 8-9).

Notice that Daniel 12 doesn't say all will be purified, but "many"—one-third according to Zechariah. The rest will die in unbelief. That purification refers to the spiritual salvation of the Jewish remnant. The "many" of Daniel 12:10 is the "all" of Romans 11:26. In the midst of abominable wickedness, God will redeem the nation Israel.

It's ironic that the Tribulation will not only be the worst of times but also issue in the best of times. The most wicked time in history will be the Tribulation, but it's also likely to be the greatest time of revival. There's no reason to think it will be more difficult for men and women to be redeemed while the world becomes more wicked. When left with nothing but evil, they will have little difficulty recognizing their sinfulness. And that is the prerequisite to salvation.

B. The Plight of the Wicked (v. 10*b*)

"The wicked shall do wickedly; and none of the wicked shall understand, but the wise shall understand."

Although great spiritual revival will occur during the Tribulation, it will also be a time when the wicked are confirmed in their wickedness. Revelation 22:11 says, "He that is filthy, let him be filthy still." Most people will continue in their gross evil, but in the midst of the furnace of affliction many will be purified like gold and silver (Zech. 13:9). Only God can take the full power of Satan's fury and turn it into revival.

The wicked won't understand the prophetic events as they unfold. They may even read the book of Daniel, but won't understand it because "the natural man [does not understand] the things of the Spirit of God" (1 Cor. 2:14). Christ said that the Father has hidden spiritual truth "from the wise and prudent, and hast revealed them unto babes" (Matt. 11:25). The human mind cannot perceive God's truth apart from enlightenment by the Holy Spirit.

## C. The Establishment of the Kingdom (vv. 11-12)

### 1. Through divine judgment (v. 11)

"From the time that the daily sacrifice shall be taken away, and the abomination that maketh desolate set up, there shall be a thousand two hundred and ninety days."

The Antichrist will make a seven-year treaty with Israel, allowing the Jewish people to worship in their Temple. However, in the middle of that period the Antichrist will put an end to their worship when he desecrates the Temple and sets up an image of himself inside it. Then begins the fiery persecution known as the Great Tribulation.

In this verse we find a different timetable regarding the end of the Tribulation. Other references mention 1,260 days or its equivalent (cf. Rev. 11:3; 12:6), but here 1,290 days are in view. Why is there an extra month?

Since the Lord just told Daniel about the purification of His people in verse 10, it's apparent that the thirty days beyond the end of the Tribulation and Christ's return will be for "the judgment of the nations" or "the judgment of the sheep and the goats" (Matt. 25:31-46). The Lord will use that time to determine who has the right to enter the Millennium and receive its blessings.

### 2. Through preliminary preparation (v. 12)

"Blessed is he that waiteth, and cometh to the thousand three hundred and five and thirty days."

After the judgment of the nations, an additional forty-five days (1,335 minus 1,290) will be needed to fully establish the millennial kingdom. If a person endured the Tribulation and was part of the remnant of sheep at Christ's right hand (Matt. 25:33), he will pass through the forty-five days and enter into the blessedness of the kingdom.

## The Blessings of the Millennial Kingdom

The Tribulation saints will enter the kingdom because they will have believed in the Lord Jesus Christ. We also will be there, returning with Christ at His second coming in our glorified bodies to reign in His kingdom. What makes it so blessed to live during the Millennium? Let look at what the Bible says:

- Christ will be ruling (Ps. 2:6).

- Satan will be captive (Rev. 20:1-3).

- The saints of the Old and New Testaments will have authority (Dan. 7:18; Matt. 19:27-28; 1 Cor. 6:2).

- Truth will dominate (Isa. 11:9).

- Righteousness will flourish (Ps. 72:7).

- Peace will reign (Isa. 2:4; 32:17).

- Joy will abound (Isa. 12:3-4; 61:3, 7).

- Justice will pervade (Isa. 11:3-4).

- The Holy Spirit's power will be revealed in its fullness (Joel 2:28).

- There will be a new Temple (Ezek. 40-48).

- The earth will be purged (Matt. 25:31-33).

- The curse will be lifted (Isa. 11:6-9).

- There will be plenty of food (Joel 2:21-27).

- Good health and healing will be abundant (Isa. 35:5-6; 65:20).

- The city of Jerusalem will be exalted (Isa. 52:1-12).

## V. THE COMMENDING OF DANIEL (v. 13)

"Go thou thy way till the end be; for thou shalt rest, and stand in thy lot at the end of the days."

This is God's blessing and promise to Daniel. Daniel was nearly ninety years old, but after living most of his life in a pagan land, he was devout, uncompromising, godly, loyal, courageous, prayerful, humble, zealous, and compassionate. He had been given thorough revelations about future Gentile kingdoms, Israel's destiny, and the frightful reign of the Antichrist during the Great Tribulation. Daniel knew that his beloved people Israel would suffer terribly, so God comforted him through the presence of the preincarnate Christ and the promise of future kingdom blessedness.

### A. His Responsibility (v. 13a)

"Go thou thy way till the end be."

The Lord was telling Daniel to remain faithful to His Word and will. That's similar to an admonition He would give centuries later: "Occupy till I come" (Luke 19:13). The apostle Peter said it like this: "Seeing, then, that all these things shall be [destroyed by divine judgment], what manner of persons ought ye to be in all holy living and godliness" (2 Pet. 3:11). Knowledge of the future brings a present responsibility to live righteously. We are to live righteously so that we will not be ashamed at Christ's return (1 John 2:28).

### B. His Resurrection (v. 13b)

"Thou shalt rest, and stand."

Daniel was to remain faithful to the time of his death. Although his body now rests in death, it will rise again. That promise is one of the great Old Testament statements about the resurrection.

## C. His Reward (v. 13c)

"[You shall] stand in thy lot at the end of the days."

The Hebrew term translated "lot" refers to an inheritance. Colossians 1:12 says the Father "hath made us fit to be partakers of the inheritance of the saints." Our heavenly Father has given us an inheritance "incorruptible, and undefiled, and that fadeth not away, reserved in heaven for [us]" (1 Pet. 1:4).

## Conclusion

It's thrilling to look at the future with the kind of hope that the Lord shared with Daniel. As Christians we don't need to worry about dying because we'll be resurrected. At the moment of physical death, our spirits go immediately to be with the Lord, so it's only our bodies that we'll wait for (2 Cor. 5:8). And in the day they rise, we'll be rewarded by the Lord. Until that time, we're responsible to continue serving the Lord.

A father was awakened in the night by his little boy. Apparently the child was having a nightmare and panicked, crying out for his daddy. As the father ran into the dark room, the boy asked, "Daddy, are you here?" "Yes, son, I'm here," the father said reassuringly. "Daddy," said the boy, "is your face looking at me?" The father answered, "Yes, son." With those words the boy lost his fear and soon fell asleep.

Our great hope for the future is knowing that the face of our Savior is looking at us. There's no need to fear the future because He's looking at us with the same love that He had for Daniel. What great confidence our Lord provides for us! As we look forward to the promises of future resurrection and eternal reward, may we accept our present responsibilities to live like Daniel.

1. What was Daniel instructed to do by shutting up the book and sealing it (Dan. 12:4; see p. 135)?
2. When will the book of Daniel be more fully understood? Why (see p. 135)?
3. Why will many be running "to and fro" during the Tribulation (12:4; see p. 136)?
4. Give evidence that the angels are as curious about the future as Daniel was (see p. 137).
5. Identify the person who was clothed in linen and standing above the river (see p. 138).
6. What is the three-and-a-half-year reign of terror designed to accomplish with regard to Israel? What will come about as a result of it (see p. 139)?
7. How did Daniel's question differ from the one the angels had asked (see p. 140)?
8. In what way was the reply Daniel received in Daniel 12:9 a source of comfort (see p. 141)?
9. Will all the nation of Israel be purified? Support your answer with Scripture. To whom does the "all Israel" of Romans 11:26 refer (see pp. 141-142)?
10. Why isn't it necessarily true that increasing wickedness will make it increasingly difficult to be redeemed? Ironically, what may be the greatest time of revival the world has ever seen (see p. 142)?
11. Why won't many of the wicked understand the spiritual significance of what will be happening during the Tribulation (1 Cor. 2:14; see p. 142)?
12. What do the thirty days beyond the 1,260 days refer to (see p. 143)?
13. What do the forty-five days beyond the 1,290 days refer to (see pp. 143-144)?
14. What are some of the blessings of the messianic kingdom (see p. 144)?
15. Explain the promises that the Lord gave to Daniel in Daniel 12:13 (see pp. 145-146).
16. What is our great hope for the future? Explain (see p. 146).

1.  Daniel's godly life is a spiritual legacy for us to follow. Undoubtedly his recording of prophecies will be instrumental in leading many to faith in Christ. What about your legacy? Are you leaving a positive, spiritual imprint on those around you? You may never write a book about spiritual things like Daniel did, but the Lord can use you to tell someone about Christ. The simple gospel you share with someone may eventually begin a ministry through that person's life that could reach thousands for Christ. So invest in others' lives and reap great spiritual dividends.

2.  Because of the wonderful future we anticipate as Christians, we should live righteously in this present life. Several verses reinforce our responsibility to be "the salt of the earth" (Matt. 5:13) rather than retreat into spiritual hibernation. Look up the following verses and identify what we are to do or be:

    *   Philippians 3:20-4:5:

    *   Colossians 4:5:

    *   1 Thessalonians 4:9-12:

    *   2 Thessalonians 3:6-13:

    *   1 Timothy 6:17-19:

    *   Titus 2:11-15; 3:1-2, 8-9:

    Did you recognize the constant theme of being both heavenly minded and earthly good? Evaluate your present ministry in light of Christ's imminent return. Are you keeping both in proper balance, or have you emphasized one more than the other?

3.  Think back through our study of Daniel 9:20-12:13. What new things have you learned about the end times? What truths in the final chapters of Daniel have made a significant impact in your life? Are you living any differently now based on what you've learned in this study?

# Scripture Index

# Topical Index

Abomination of desolation. *See* Temple, the

Ahasuerus, reign of, 78

Alexander the Great, reign of, 78-81

Anderson, Sir Robert, on Daniel's seventy weeks, 30-35

Angels
demonic obstruction of, 68-72
Gabriel. *See* Gabriel
messenger ministry of, 14-17
Michael. *See* Michael
speed of, 14

Antichrist, the
character of, 97-102
deeds of, 52-56, 103-8
God's tolerance of, 99, 111
judgment of, 108-9
people of, 45
perversion of, 100-1
timing of, 95-97
titles of, 45, 97

Antiochus Epiphanes, reign of, 85-89

Antiochus the Great, reign of, 81-84

Anti-Semitism. *See* Israel, history of, persecution of
Arabs, end-time warfare of the, 105-9

Armageddon, Battle of, 103-9

Atheism, social acceptance of, 101

Calendar, biblical. *See* Years, reckoning of biblical

Chastening, responding to divine, 91-92

China, end-time warfare of, 108

Daniel
accuracy of the book of, 77
commending of, 145-48
God's love for, 16
disappointment of, 60-63
prayers of, 11-14, 60-63, 73-74
resurrection of, 145
understanding the book of, 134-36

Demons, world power of, 69-72. *See also* Warfare, spiritual

Discipline, responding to divine. *See* Chastening

Eschatology. *See* Antichrist; Armageddon; Israel; Messiah; Millennial kingdom; Prophecy; Rome, revived empire of; Tribulation

155